TRIUMPH
OVER
TEMPTATION

JOHN OWEN

TRIUMPH
OVER
TEMPTATION

PURSUING A LIFE OF PURITY

INTRODUCTION BY

J. I. PACKER

EDITED BY

JAMES M. HOUSTON

Victor®

The Bible Teacher's Teacher

COOK COMMUNICATIONS MINISTRIES
Colorado Springs, Colorado • Paris, Ontario
KINGSWAY COMMUNICATIONS LTD
Eastbourne, England

Victor® is an imprint of
Cook Communications Ministries, Colorado Springs, CO 80918
Cook Communications, Paris, Ontario
Kingsway Communications, Eastbourne, England

TRIUMPH OVER TEMPTATION
Copyright © 2005 by James M. Houston
Copyright © 1983 as SIN AND TEMPTATION by James M. Houston

Cover Design by: Jackson Design CO, LLC/Greg Jackson

First Printing, 2005
Printed in United States of America

2 3 4 5 6 7 8 9 10

First published 1983 by Multnomah Press, Portland, Oregon 97266 U.S.A.

This edition of *Triumph Over Temptation* is compiled from the three treatises *Of the
Mortification of Sin in Believers; Of Temptation;* and *The Nature, Power Deceit and
Prevalency of Indwelling Sin;* and is based upon William H. Goold's edition of
1850–1853.

Scripture references in this volume are either directly quoted from the *King James
Version* or are a paraphrase of that version by John Owen.

Library of Congress Cataloging-in-Publication Data

Owen, John, 1616-1683.
  [Sin & temptation]
  Triumph over temptation : the challenge of personal godliness / John Owen ;
abridged and edited by James M. Houston ; introduction by J.I. Packer.

      p. cm. -- (Victor classics)
  Originally published: Sin & temptation. Portland, Or. : Multnomah Press, 1983, in
series: Classics of faith and devotion.

  Includes bibliographical references and indexes.
  ISBN 978-0-7814-4172-8 (pbk.)
  1. Sin. 2. Temptation. 3. Christian life. I. Houston, J. M. (James Macintosh), 1922-
II. Title. III. Series.
  BT715.O932 2005
  241'.3--dc22
                        2004025500

Dr. James M. Houston was born to missionary parents who served in Spain. Dr. Houston served as university lecturer at Oxford University, England, from 1949 to 1971. He was a Fellow of Hertford College during the period between 1964 and 1971, and held the office of Principal of Regent College from 1969 to 1978. He has served as Chancellor of Regent College and is currently Emeritus Professor of Spiritual Theology.

Dr. Houston has been active in the establishment and encouragement of lay training centers across the continents. These include the C. S. Lewis Institute in Washington, D.C., and The London Institute for the Study of Contemporary Christianity. In addition to his work with the classics series, he has published several books.

CONTENTS

*Sin indwells all believers. It is a law within our hearts. We
never finish dealing with it, even as Christians.*

*Sin is enmity toward God. It is aversion of God, and it is
opposed to anything we do for Him. A humble walk before God
is necessary.*

*Sin proceeds in temptation by steps. The first step of temptation
is to deceive the mind. Meditation and prayer weaken deceit,
but sin seeks to divert believers from these duties.*

*The second step of temptation is to entice the emotions. We
must guard our affections by mortifying sin and fixing our
affections on the cross of Christ.*

*The third step of temptation is to conceive sin in the will. Sin
uses the deception of the mind and the enticement of the emotions to accomplish this conception. God acts to prevent the
fruition of sin by His providence and grace.*

PART II: TEMPTATION OF BELIEVERS

PART III: MORTIFICATION OF SIN IN BELIEVERS

God commands all believers to mortify the deeds of the body through the Spirit. He accompanies this command with the promise of abundant life. Mortification involves the habitual weakening of, and contention against, sin.

We need to mortify besetting sins daily. The Holy Spirit alone performs this work in believers. Mortification is not possible for unregenerate men or for disobedient believers.

Nine considerations aid believers in preparing for the mortification of sin. Believers should realize the guilt, danger, and evil of sin. We should also meditate on God's perfection in contrast to our sinfulness.

The work of mortification actually involves only two things. First, we must trust in Christ's sufficiency. Second, we must seek the Holy Spirit, who alone mortifies sin.

PREFACE TO VICTOR CLASSICS

With the profusion of books now being published, most Christian readers require some guidance for a basic collection of spiritual works that will remain lifelong companions. This new series of Victor Classics is being edited to provide just such a basic library for the home. Those selected may not all be commonly known today, but each has a central concern of relevance for the contemporary Christian.

Another goal for this collection of books is a reawakening. It is a reawakening to the spiritual thoughts and meditations of the forgotten centuries. Many Christians today have no sense of the past. If the Reformation is important to them, they jump from the apostolic Church to the sixteenth century, forgetting some fourteen centuries of the work of the Holy Spirit among many devoted to Christ. These classics will remove that gap and enrich their readers by the faith and devotion of God's saints through all history.

And so we turn to the books, and to their purpose. Some books have changed the lives of their readers. Notice how Athanasius's *Life of Antony* affected Augustine or William Law's *A Serious Call to a Devout and Holy Life* influenced John Wesley. Others, such as Augustine's *Confessions* or Thomas à Kempis's *Imitation of Christ*, have remained perennial sources of inspiration throughout the ages. We sincerely hope those selected in this series will have a like effect on our readers.

Each one of the classics chosen for this series is deeply significant to a contemporary Christian leader. In some cases, the thoughts and reflections of the classic writer are mirrored in the leader's genuine ambitions and desires today, an unusual pairing of hearts and minds across the centuries. And thus these individuals have been asked to write the introduction on the book that has been so meaningful to his or her own life.

EDITING THE CLASSICS

Such classics of spiritual life have had their obstacles. Their original language, the archaic style of later editions, their length, the digressions, the allusions to by-gone cultures—all make the use of them discouraging to the modern reader. To reprint them (as was done on a massive scale in the last century and still so today) does not overcome these handicaps of style, length, and language. To seek the kernel and remove the husk, this series involves therefore the abridging, rewriting, and editing of each book. At the same time we sought to keep to the essential message given in the work, and to pursue as much as possible the author's original style.

The principles of editing are as follows. Keep sentences short. Paragraphs are also shortened. Material is abridged where there are digressions or allusions made that are time-binding. Archaic words are altered. Spelling is that of Webster's Dictionary. Logical linkage may have to be added to abridged material. The identity of theme or argument is kept sharply in mind. Allusions to other authors are given brief explanation.

For the Christian, the Bible is the basic text for spiritual reading. All other devotional reading is secondary and should never be a substitute for it. Therefore, the allusions to Scripture in the Victor Classics are searched out and referenced in the text. This is where other editions of these books may ignore the scriptural quality of these works, which are inspired and guided by the Bible. The biblical focus is always the hallmark of truly Christian spirituality.

PURPOSE FOR THE CLASSICS: SPIRITUAL READING

Since our sensate and impatient culture makes spiritual reading strange and difficult for us, the reader should be cautioned to read these books slowly, meditatively, and reflectively. One cannot rush through them like a detective story. In place of novelty, they focus on remembrance, reminding us of values that remain of eternal consequence. We may enjoy many new things, but values are as old as God's creation.

The goal for the reader of these books is not to seek information. Instead, these volumes teach one about living wisely. That takes obedience, submission of will, change of heart, and a tender, docile spirit. When John the Baptist saw Jesus, he reacted, "He must increase, and I must decrease." Likewise, spiritual reading decreases our natural instincts, to allow His love to increase within us.

Nor are these books "how-to" kits or texts. They take us as we are—that is, as persons, and not as functionaries. They guide us to *be* authentic, and not necessarily to help us to promote more professional activities. Such books require us to make time for their slow digestion, space to let their thoughts enter into our hearts, and discipline to let new insights "stick" and become part of our Christian character.

—James M. Houston

EDITOR'S NOTE ABOUT JOHN OWEN AND THE RELEVANCE OF THIS CLASSIC

Our times have been called the "me generation" because of the psychological cult of self-fulfilment and its accompanying narcissism. We live in a society that is deaf to a well-known psychologist's question, "Whatever happened to sin?" O. Herbert Mowrer has written candidly about this:

> For several decades we psychologists looked upon the whole matter of sin and moral accountability as a great incubus, and acclaimed our liberation from it as epoch making. But at length we have discovered that to be "free" in this sense, that is to have the excuse of being "sick" rather than sinful, is to court the danger of also being lost.[1]

We are beginning to see once more that there can be no recovery of self-realization—as the story of the prodigal son reminds us—without the recovery of moral responsibility. For this to happen, sin must be recovered once more in our generation. Casual, superficial Christian beliefs will not do so. We must listen to texts like John Owen's *Indwelling Sin in Believers.* It is crucial, therefore, that this essay and two others on the same theme be re-presented to this generation.

TRIUMPH OVER TEMPTATION

THE MAN

John Owen was born in 1616 and died in 1683. He lived through all the troubled times of the Civil War in England, the execution of Charles I, the war in Ireland, the Restoration, and the persecution of Nonconformism. He suffered poor health, and his own private life was checkered.

A leader of the Congregationalists, Owen was perhaps the greatest of the Puritan scholars. He was successively a chaplain to several wealthy families, Cromwell's chaplain in Ireland, dean of Christ Church of Oxford, and vice-chancellor of Oxford University. He had a high ambition for England: he wanted a Parliament composed of godly men to rule the country. As a pastor, preacher, and theologian, he had national recognition, and he was admired by his friends as "the Calvin of England."

Owen ranks high in the history of the Christian Church. His five-volume work on the Holy Spirit is the most outstanding English contribution to this subject ever written in systematic theology. His exegesis of the Epistle to the Hebrews is likewise a great work.

THIS BOOK

In devotional and practical theology, John Owen wrote several important treatises. It is out of this latter category that we have chosen the three works that make up this present volume.

The first of the treatises to be published was *Of the Mortification of Sin in Believers* (1656). It was compiled from university sermons that Owen delivered every other week at Oxford while dean of Christ Church (1651–57) and vice-chancellor of Oxford University.

Friends urged Owen to publish other sermon material, *Of Temptation*, in 1658. During this time divisions were splitting and weakening the Puritan rule in England. Three disturbances led to the Restoration two years later. The need for personal godliness in such times motivated Owen to compose this essay.

The third treatise, *The Nature, Power, Deceit, and Prevalency of Indwelling Sin*, was written in 1667 when Owen and his friends were suffering from the repression of Nonconformism in England. On one visit to Oxford, Owen narrowly escaped arrest and imprisonment. While "lying low," he spent time writing this and other works.

The reality of indwelling sin in Christians had no doubt come to Owen with overwhelming conviction during the last years of the Commonwealth government. He resisted Cromwell's personal ambitions to be crowned king and faced dissensions and strife among his compatriots. Later he lived to see his and others' dreams for "a commonwealth of godliness" collapse. All the political aspirations Owen had for his nation burst like soap bubbles. He saw clearly that the reality behind it all was indwelling sin in Christians.

Perhaps we shall also live to experience similar disillusionment, due to our churches' neglect of the reality of sin's abode in human hearts.

These three treatises reveal a remarkable and deep insight into the workings and motives of the human heart. Owen's search is always exhaustive. His humility is always discerning. And his acceptance of the authority of the Scriptures is powerful.

HIS WRITING

In this rewritten and somewhat abridged form of his three treatises, care has been taken to preserve the flavor and style of John
Owen. But his thoughts are more massively than elegantly
expressed. His language is latinized in style, repetitive in its
drive to explore exhaustively, and confusing in the enumeration
of the many headings, subheadings, and major and minor
points. This gives a turgidity to his unabridged writings and
only an enthusiast can work his way through them.

The text has been rewritten from that edited by William H.
Goold from 1850 to 1853. The liberties taken with the text have
been guided by the attitude described in that edition.

> Where shall we find in the theological writings of his
> [Owen's] own or of any age, so much of the accumulated
> treasures of sanctified learning—of the mind of God clearly
> elucidated and invincibly defended—or [of such] profound
> and massive thought? His works are like a soil which is lit-
> erally impregnated with gold and in which burnished
> masses of the native ore are sure to reward him who
> patiently labors in it.[2]

It is hoped that some of the stones and gravel have been
washed out to let the modem reader pick out more quickly and
appreciatively his many nuggets of pure gold.

The editors suggest that Owen's work can be more readily
appreciated when read aloud because Owen, at heart, was a
preacher rather than a writer. This exercise will bring to life his
words and help the truth of his essays become lucid.

We are grateful to Dr. J. I. Packer for his introductory essay on

Owen. This endorsement by such a highly respected theologian of the English-speaking world testifies to the great benefits obtainable from the resources of John Owen. It is fitting that Dr. Packer should tell us why Owen is still important for all of us to discover.

NOTES

[1] Herbert Mowrer, "Sin, the Lesser of Two Evils," *American Psychologist* XV (1960): 301–304.

[2] A. Chalmers, *Life of Owen* (1850).

INTRODUCTION

I've been reading a friend of yours," said a young man last Sunday as we left church. He chuckled. "I think he knows me."

"Who is it?" I asked.

"John Owen. He seems to know exactly what's going on inside me and what I'm going to think next. He's great."

I thought of the way Owen had ministered to me across the centuries in 1947, saving my spiritual sanity when a certain type of holiness teaching had almost destroyed it. I knew what the young man meant.

Owen died more than 320 years ago, in 1683. All his works are in print today, and those who know him regard him as perhaps the greatest of all English theologians. Who was he, and what is the secret of his continuing influence on those who read him?

He was born in 1616. He entered Queen's College, Oxford, at the age of twelve and took his M.A. in 1635. Driven by ambition, he studied hard. In his early twenties, however, conviction of sin threw him into such turmoil that for three months he could scarcely utter a coherent sentence on anything. Slowly he learned to trust Christ and so found peace. In 1637 he left the university for reasons of conscience and became a pastor. In the 1640s he was chaplain to Oliver Cromwell and in 1651 was made dean of Christ Church, Oxford's largest college. The following year he became vice-chancellor and reorganized the university with conspicuous success. After 1660 he led the Independents through

Trusting Christ is the only way to Peace!

the bitter years of persecution. He was offered the presidency of Harvard, but declined. He was a martyr to asthma and gall-stones for years before he died.

He was a theologian of vast learning and organizing power. His thoughts were not subtle or complicated. Like Norman pillars, they leave in the mind an impression of massive grandeur precisely because of their solid simplicity. In protest against the self-conscious literary posturing of the age, he was careless in presentation, yet he was always thorough and exact in formulation. He wrote for readers who, once they take up a subject, cannot rest till they see to the bottom of it and who find exhaustiveness not exhausting but refreshing. His books have been truly described as a series of theological systems, each organized round a different center. Never would he isolate parts from the whole.

Owen embodied all that was noblest in Puritan devotion. "Holiness," said his junior colleague David Clarkson in the sermon preached at Owen's burial, "gave a divine lustre to his other accomplishments." He was humble. "There are two things that are suited to humble the souls of men," he wrote, "… a due consideration of God, and then of ourselves. Of God, in His greatness, glory, holiness, power, majesty, and authority; of ourselves, in our mean, abject, and sinful condition."[1] The latter is important, for "the man that understands the evil of his own heart, how vile it is, is the only useful, fruitful, and solidly believing and obedient person."[2]

Owen himself had learned that a man must abhor himself before he can serve God aright. Again, Owen knew the power of his own message. Preachers, he held (and he identified himself always as a preacher), need "experience of the power of the truth which they preach in and upon their own souls. ... A man preacheth that sermon only well unto others which preacheth itself in

I am no preacher except to myself.
I must preach to myself every day!

his own soul."[3] Therefore "I hold myself bound in conscience
and in honor, not even to imagine that I have attained a proper *Really*
knowledge of any one article of truth, much less to publish it, *Believing*
unless through the Holy Spirit I have had such a taste of it, in its *Comes*
spiritual sense, that I may be able, from the heart, to say with the *Comes*
psalmist, 'I have believed, and therefore have I spoken.'"[4] Hence *from the heart*
the authority and skill with which Owen probes the dark depths
of the human heart. "Whole passages flash upon the mind of the
reader," wrote Andrew Thomson of *Temptation*, "with an
influence that makes him feel as if they had been written for himself alone." When more than a century ago the famous "Rabbi"
Duncan told his students to read *Indwelling Sin*, he added: "But
prepare for the knife."

Owen wrote in a latinized English style, fluent and stately,
though cumbersome by ordinary standards. His prose is best
read aloud; then its rhetorical force comes through. Those who
think as they read find his expansiveness suggestive and his
fullness fertilizing. "Owen is said to be prolix," wrote Spurgeon,
"but it would be truer to say that he is condensed. His style is
heavy because he gives notes of what he might have said, and
passes on without fully developing the great thoughts of his
capacious mind. He requires hard study, and none of us ought to
grudge it."

Owen preached and wrote his theology in the service of religion (that is, Christian godliness), and the living of the Christian
life was his constant theme, just as it was Calvin's (a thinker, inci-
dentally, whom Owen much resembled). In dealing with the
Christian life, Owen constantly reminds the Christian of four
things.

First, he is a *man*, created in God's image for rational action
and equipped to that end with a trinity of faculties: understanding, will, and affection. (a) "The mind or understanding is the

Peter
Connover
—Shin

Chris Fletcher
—finger 23

I have
a mind
a heart
and
emotions

As a Human I
am made to be
rational.

[handwritten note top left: understanding always comes first.]

[handwritten note top right: my will follows and is guided by understanding]

leading faculty of the soul; ... its office is to guide, direct, choose; ... it is the eye of the soul."[5] (b) As the mind is a power of apprehension, so the will is a power of action: "a rational appetite: rational as guided by the mind, and an appetite as excited by the affections.... It chooseth nothing but ... as it hath an appearance of good."[6] (c) The category of affection covers the various emotional drives, positive and negative, that elicit choices by drawing us to or repelling us from particular objects. No choice is ever made without some degree of affection. Therefore "affections are in the soul as the helm is in the ship; if it be laid hold on by a skillful hand, he turneth the whole vessel which way he pleaseth.... It is vain to contend with anything that hath the power of our affections in its disposal; it will prevail at the last."[7]

Man was made to know good with his mind, to desire it with his affections once he knows it, and to cleave to it with his will once he has felt its attraction. Accordingly God, who is the supreme good, moves man not by direct action on the affections or will, but by addressing His speech to man's mind, so bringing to bear on him the force of truth. Scripture is God's speech, given us in the form of human speech; so the preacher's first task must be to teach the contents of the Bible, and the Christian's first task must be to learn them.

[handwritten note: I must learn truth before I can love it!!!]

Second, the Christian is a *fallen* man, a sinner. Sin has alienated him both from God and from himself, and though as a Christian he is a forgiven sinner, the marks of sin are still on him. Sin disorders the soul and disintegrates the character: "The faculties move cross and contrary one to another; the will chooseth not the good which the mind discovers.... Commonly the affections ... get the sovereignty, and draw the whole soul captive after them."[8] Fallen man is no longer rational, but unstable, inconstant, distracted by conflicting passions and blind impulses, and gripped by the lust to disobey. Of indwelling sin in Christians

[handwritten note bottom left: whatever masters my affections masters me!]

[handwritten note bottom right: my affections must be won!]

my affections are my drives + impulses

I will control my whole life if I control my affections

Owen wrote: "Its nature and formal design is to oppose God; God as lawgiver, God as holy, God as the author of the gospel, a way of salvation by grace and not by works, are the direct objects of the law of sin."[9]

The sin nature of man corrupts everything: mind, will, + affection.

Ungodliness, unrighteousness, unbelief, and heresy are sin's natural forms of self-expression. Sin pervades and pollutes the whole man: "It adheres as a depraved principle unto our minds, in darkness and vanity; unto our affections in sensuality; unto our wills, in a loathing of, and aversion from, that which is good; and ... is continually putting itself upon us, in inclinations, motions, or suggestions, to evil."[10] It resists the work of grace from first to last: "When Christ comes with His spiritual power upon the soul to conquer it to Himself, He hath no quiet landing place. He can set foot upon no ground but what he must fight for."[11]

Sin sticks in my head, makes me love what is wrong, and makes me choose evil.

Christian living must therefore be founded on self-abhorrence and self-distrust because of indwelling sin's presence and power. "Constant self-abasement, condemnation, and abhorrency is another duty that is directly opposed unto the ... rule of sin in the soul. No frame of mind is a better antidote against the poison of sin.... It is the soil wherein all grace will thrive and flourish.... To keep our souls in a constant state of mourning and self-abasement is the most necessary part of our wisdom ... and it is so far from having any inconsistency with those consolations and joys, which the gospel tenders unto us in believing, as that it is the only way to let them into the soul in a due manner."[12]

Christ died to make us free, lives to make us free

Third, the Christian is a redeemed man. Christ died to deliver him from sin's guilt and now lives to save him from its power. As redemption by Christ is the heart of Christian doctrine, so faith in and love for Christ must be the heart of Christian religion. "They know nothing of the life and power of the gospel, nothing of the reality of the grace of God, nor do they believe

self-abasement, condemnation, and abhorrence are the proper mindsets for victory over sin!

[handwritten top margin: Christ is only loving towards the christian — "God is love!" — only for the believer.]

[handwritten: only Christ's love can win my affections from sin!]

aright one article of the Christian faith, whose hearts are not sensible of the love of Christ therein. Nor is he sensible of the love of Christ whose affections are not thereon drawn out unto him. I say, they make a pageant of religion ... whose hearts are not really affected with the love of Christ, in the susception and discharge of the work of mediation, so as to have real and spiritually sensible affections for Him. Men ... have no real acquaintance with Christianity who imagine that the placing of the most intense affections of our souls on the person of Christ, the loving Him with all our hearts because of His love, our being overcome thereby, until we are sick of love, the constant motions of our souls towards Him with delight and adherence, are but fancies and imaginations."[13]

[handwritten: Do I really know the love of God in Christ? Wouldn't I be different?]

Fourth, the Christian is a *regenerate* man, a new creation in Christ. A new principle of life (awareness of, desire for, and responsiveness to God) and a new habit of obedience to God's law have been implanted in him. This is the prophesied "circumcision of the heart." "Whereas the blindness, obstinacy, and stubbornness in sin that is in us by nature, with the prejudices which possess our minds and affections, hinder us from conversion unto God; by this circumcision they are taken away"[14]—and conscious conversion, at least in the case of an adult, follows at once. From then on his heart is a battlefield, where "the flesh" (the "old man") tirelessly disputes the supremacy of "the spirit" (the "new man"). Sin, from which the Christian formally dissociated himself in his initial repentance, seems to take on a life of its own. Paul likens it, so Owen tells us, "to a person, a living person, called 'the old man,' with his faculties and properties, his wisdom, craft, subtlety, strength."[15]

[handwritten: It is like a whole nother person inside me.]

Sin is always at work in the heart; a temporary lull in its assaults means not that it is dead, but that it is very much alive. "Sin is never less quiet, than when it seems to be most quiet, and

[handwritten left margin: I am under new ownership]

[handwritten bottom margin: Is my heart circumcised? Are my affections, mind, and will owned by God?]

[handwritten marginal notes at top: "my will has to be replaced by christ's will — my affections have to be replaced by christ's affections"; "my mind has to be replaced by christ's mind."]

[handwritten note in left margin: "my enemy is always plotting my death."]

its waters are for the most part deep, when they are still."[16] Sin's strategy is to induce a false sense of security as a prelude to a surprise attack. "By sin we are oftentimes, ere we are aware, carried into distempered affections, foolish imaginations, and pleasing delightfulness in things that are not good nor profitable.... When the soul is doing ... quite another thing ... sin starts that in the heart ... that carries it away into that which is evil and sinful. Yea, to manifest its power, sometimes when the soul is seriously engaged in the mortification of any sin, it will ... lead it away into alliance with that very sin whose ruin it is seeking.... I know no greater burden in the life of a believer than these involuntary surprisals.... And it is in respect unto them, that the apostle makes his complaint [in] Romans 7:24."[17] *[handwritten: "Sin will sometime outcraft me!"]*

The battle is lifelong. "Sometimes a soul thinks or hopes that it may through grace be utterly freed from this troublesome inmate. Upon some sweet enjoyment of God, some full supply of grace, some return from wandering, some deep affliction, some thorough humiliation, the soul begins to hope that it shall now be freed from the law of sin. But after a while ... sin acts again, makes good its old station,"[17] and the fight has to be resumed. No one "gets out of Romans 7" in this world.

Viewed from God's standpoint, the Christian life is a matter of progressive sanctification. "Sanctification is an immediate work of the Spirit of God on the souls of believers, purifying and cleansing of their natures from the pollution and uncleanness of sin, renewing in them the image of God, and thereby enabling them from a spiritual and habitual principle of grace, to yield obedience unto God. ... Or more briefly; it is the universal renovation of our natures by the Holy Spirit into the image of God, through Jesus Christ. Hence it follows that our holiness, which is the fruit and effect of this work ... as it compriseth the renewed ... image of God wrought in us, so it consists in a holy obedience

27

Sanctification is 24/7, 365 days a year
sin takes no holidays!

unto God, by Jesus Christ, according to the terms of the covenant of grace."[19] Christian holiness is "the implanting, writing, and realizing of the gospel in our souls ... the word changed into grace in our hearts. ... Growth is nothing but ... increase in conformity to that word."[20]

The positive side of sanctification is that it brings to life the new powers and inclinations that regeneration implanted within us. "Frequency of acts doth naturally increase and strengthen the habits whence they proceed. And in spiritual habits (e.g., faith, hope, love), it is so, moreover, by God's appointment.... They grow and thrive in and by their exercise.... The want thereof is the principal means of their decay."[21] The Christian, therefore, must use the means of grace assiduously, hearing, reading, meditating, watching, praying, worshiping; he must animate himself to "universal obedience," an all-round, all-day conformity to God's revealed will; and he must persevere in it with resolution and resilience. *Sanctification is not a one time transaction!*

Yet the believer must remember that the power is from God, not himself, and do it all in a spirit of prayerful dependence, or else he will fail. For "the actual aid, assistance and internal operation of the Spirit of God is necessary ... unto producing of every holy act of our minds, wills, and affections, in every duty whatsoever.... Notwithstanding the power or ability which believers have received by habitual grace, they still stand in need of actual grace in ... every single ... act or duty towards God."[22] This help will be withheld from those who forget their need of it and never ask for it. *Sanctification is moment by moment!!!*

The negative side of sanctification is mortifying sin. This is more than the suppressing or counteracting of sinful impulse; it is nothing less than progressively eradicating it. "Mortify" means "kill," and "the end aimed at in this duty is destruction, as it is in all killing: the utter ruin, destruction and gradual annihilation of all

[Handwritten note top right: Sin has been killed by Christ still needs to be killed?]

the remainders of this cursed life of sin."[23] Indwelling sin has been dethroned and dealt its death blow through the believer's union with Christ in His death. Now, with the Spirit's aid, the Christian must spend his lifetime draining sin's lifeblood. We may not relax, for sin "will no otherwise die, but by being gradually and constantly weakened; spare it, and it heals its wounds, and recovers strength."[24] *[Handwritten: Don't take your hand of sins neck!]*

Mortification, which "consists in a constant taking part with grace ... against the principle, acts, and fruits of sin,"[25] is often painful and unattractive; Christ compared it to plucking out an eye or cutting off a limb; but it is one aspect of the way of life that no Christian dare neglect. How in detail it is to be done is explained in Owen's treatise, reprinted in this book.

[Handwritten margin note: I cannot deal peaceably with sin! murder, assassination cur is the only ensure]

Owen's overall view of the inside story of each Christian's life, as summarized above, is the frame of reference within which the three works that follow should be read. *Indwelling Sin* (1667) seems to me to be in a class by itself in its power to make Christians see what goes on inside them as the drama of grace-versus-sin unfolds. *Temptation* (1658) supplements the analysis with similar searching effect, and *Mortification* (1656; second enlarged edition, 1658) follows on with a masterful battle strategy. All three studies are Bible based: Owen merely echoes what he finds Scripture saying and offers Scripture proof for every point he makes. All three are spiritually profound: Owen's insight into the human heart is nothing short of uncanny, as is his power to communicate that insight in what at first seems a colorless, lumbering style of utterance. And all three (so it seems to me) call for our attention today.

If our concern is with the burgeoning theological study of spirituality, a Puritan model of godliness will highlight for us aspects of spiritual reality that the better-known models—patristic, medieval, sixteenth-century, eighteenth-century, twentieth-century, Roman

Catholic, Orthodox, Anglican, Wesleyan, Lutheran, Reformed—do not focus so clearly; and there is no doubt that among all the Puritan models Owen's is the richest. If our concern is with practical Christian living today, a Puritan model of godliness will most quickly expose the reason why our current spirituality is shallow, namely the shallowness of our views of sin. And there is no question that among all the Puritan models, Owen's goes deepest at this point and can make us realistic about sin most speedily. Christians today badly need what Owen has to give us. May we be enabled to see that.

It should not be thought that this present volume sets before us the whole of Owen's view of the Christian life, or even half of it. His treatment of sin and temptation is only one strand in the thick rope of his total spiritual teaching. To get its full measure, one would have to study at least his programmatic discourse *Of Communion with God the Father, Son and Holy Ghost, each person distinctly, in love, grace and consolation;* or *The Saint's Fellowship with the Father, Son and Holy Ghost, unfolded* (1657); also his glowing treatment of devotion to Jesus Christ in *The Glory of Christ* (1684 and 1691); also his monumental *Pneumatologia: a Discourse on the Holy Spirit* (1674), with supplementary discourses on *Causes, Ways and Means of Understanding the Mind of God* (1678) and *The Work of the Spirit as a Comforter* (1693); also his treatment of *Spiritual-Mindedness* (on meditation: 1681); and of *Psalm 130* (on knowledge of God's forgiveness: 1668); also *The True Nature of a Gospel Church* (1689), where Owen fills in the corporate context that is integral to true personal devotion.

The fact is that in spirituality, as in other branches of theology, Owen is to be bracketed with such as Augustine, Luther, Calvin, Edwards, Spurgeon, and Lloyd-Jones: he is one of the all-time masters. In his own day, and among eighteenth- and nineteenth-century evangelicals, his stature was known. It was left to the twentieth century to forget it: but, though that century is now through, there is still an opportunity to regain and assimilate knowledge of Owen as the twenty-first century opens. If in our own "breaking times" (a Puritan phrase) we allow Owen to strengthen our grasp of the things that abide, knowledge of which upheld him through his own "breaking times" of civil war, anarchy, and persecution,[26] we shall do well. The selections that follow make an excellent starting point.

The proof of the pudding is, of course, in the eating. And for that reason I should perhaps end by saying a little more about the benefit that I myself have gained from Owen's devotional theology that I have been recommending so highly. I have in fact benefited from a great deal more of Owen's literary legacy than the devotional material. It was Owen's *Death of Death in the Death of Christ* that in 1953 showed me that the habitual form of biblical testimony to the atonement is particularistic, thus turning me from a four-point into a five-point Calvinist. It was Owen's *Pneumatologia* that gave me my present understanding of the way to relate regeneration and conversion. And Owen's *True Nature of a Gospel Church*, along with his *Discourse on Spiritual Gifts* and *The Nature of Apostacy*, have done more over the years than any other books to shape my thoughts on what local church life should be. A learned friend who became a seminary professor used to refer to me during the fifties as an Owenian, and I could not deny the justice of the ascription. But at present I am only concerned with Owen's devotional teaching, particularly that reproduced in this volume. I said earlier that it saved my sanity. Let me explain how.

I was converted—that is, as I now see it, I came to Jesus Christ in a decisive commitment, needing and seeking God's forgiveness and acceptance, and assured of Christ's redeeming love for me and His personal call to me—in my first university term. The group that took responsibility for my nurture as a Christian was heavily pietistic in tone and outlook, and it left me in no doubt that for me, as a Christian, the most important thing henceforth was the quality of my walk with God. In the familiar small-minority manner the group was decidedly elitist in spirit, holding that only Bible-believing evangelicals could say anything worth hearing about the Christian life, and conversely that whatever evangelicals who were thought sound enough to address the group might say about the Christian life was bound to be good.

Having absorbed this elitism by osmosis as new converts absorb things, I listened with great expectation and excitement to the preachers and teachers whom the group brought in week by week, viewing them as undoubtedly the top devotional instructors in the country. Also, I read widely in the devotional literature that the group approved. While highly critical of other forms of Christianity (not, I think, without reason, but certainly without proper humility and respect), I drank up all that came to me from these approved sources as being in truth oracles from God. Had I not taken it all so seriously my traumas would have been less.

Whether what I thought I heard was what was really said may be left an open question, but what I thought I was being told was this. There are two sorts of Christians, first class and second class, "spiritual" and "carnal" (a distinction drawn from 1 Cor. 3:1–3). The former know sustained peace and joy, constant inner confidence and regular victory over temptation and sin, in a way that the latter do not. Anyone who hopes to be of any use to God must first be "spiritual" in the stated sense. As a lonely, dithery adolescent introvert whose newfound assurance had not changed his temperament overnight, I had to conclude that the reality of "spiritual" experience was not yet mine; yet I certainly hoped to be useful to God. So what was I to do?

The message as received continued as follows, speaking to that question. There is a secret of rising from carnality to spirituality, a secret mirrored in the maxim: Let go and let God. This secret has to do with becoming Spirit filled. The Spirit-filled man is taken out of the second half of Romans 7 (the experience of constant moral defeat through self-reliance) into the sunshine of Romans 8 where he walks in the Spirit and is not so defeated. (Let me say that I do not now accept this understanding of Romans 7, or of the relation between Romans 7 and 8, or of the quality of experience to which Romans 8 points; to be honest, I now see it as a pietistic exegetical freak; in those days, however, it was the only view of the matter I had met. But to continue.) The secret of being Spirit filled, so I gathered, is twofold.

To start with, one must *deny self*. It seems clear to me now that when Jesus called for self-denial, He meant the negating of *carnal* self—that is to say self-will; self-assertion; the Adamic syndrome; the sinful, egocentric behavior pattern that one has been developing from birth; the recurring irrational impulse to do anything rather than obey God and embrace what one knows to be right.

But what I seemed to hear then was a summons to deny personal self, thereby opening the door to being taken over by Jesus Christ in such a way that my present experience of thinking and willing would become something different, an experience of Christ Himself living in me, animating me, and doing the thinking and choosing for me. Put like that, of course, it sounds more like the formula of demon possession than the ministry of the indwelling Christ according to the New Testament. But in those days I knew nothing about demon possession, and what I have just verbalized seemed to be the plain meaning of "I live; yet not I, but Christ liveth in me" (Gal. 2:20 KJV) as explained by the approved speakers. We used to sing this chorus:

O to be saved from myself, dear Lord,
O to be lost in Thee;
O that it may be no more I
But Christ who lives in me!

Whatever its author may have meant, I sang it wholeheartedly in the sense spelled out above.

Part two of the secret, the positive counterpart of self-denial, was *consecration* and *faith*. Consecration meant total self-surrender, laying one's all on the altar, handing over every part of one's life to the lordship of Jesus Christ. Nowadays I perceive this as another name for that outliving of repentance that the gospel requires of Christians as such, but then I saw it, as I am sure I was encouraged to see it, as part of the special technique for entry into the higher form of Christian experience. Through consecration one would be emptied of self, and the empty vessel would then automatically be filled with the Spirit so that Christ's full power within one would be ready for use. It did not occur to me then, as it has done since, to wonder whether imagery that seems to come from the world of charging batteries, draining and replenishing receptacles, and switching on the electricity, is really apt for expressing the Holy Spirit's personal ministry.

With consecration was to go faith, which as explained by them meant looking to the indwelling Christ moment by moment, not only to do one's thinking and choosing in one and for one, but also one's fighting and resisting of temptation. Rather than meet temptation directly (which would be fighting in one's own strength), one should hand it over to Christ to deal with and expect Him to banish it. I nowadays think that the way to deal with temptation is at once to say no and with that to ask the Lord for strength to keep saying no and actually to mortify—that is, do to death, squelch, and enervate—the sinful urge. Then, however, I simply tried to practice the consecration and faith technique as I had understood it—heap powerful magic, as I supposed, the precious secret of victorious living.

But I did not get on well at all. I scraped my inside, figuratively speaking, to find things to yield to the Lord so as to make consecration complete, and I worked hard to "let go and let God" when temptation made its presence felt. At that time I did not know that Harry Ironside, sometime pastor of Moody Memorial Church, Chicago, once drove himself into a full-scale mental breakdown through trying to find the secret that I was trying to find in the way that I was trying to find it. Nor did I then conclude, as I have concluded since, that the higher Christian life as I was conceiving it is an unreality, a will-o'-the-wisp that no one has ever laid hold of at all, and that those who testify to their experience in these terms really, if unwittingly, distort what has happened to them.

All I knew was that the expected experience was not coming, the technique was not working. And since according to the teaching everything depended on consecration being total, the fault must lie in me. So I must scrape my inside yet again to find whatever maggots of unconsecrated selfhood still lurked there. A few months of this left me, as can be imagined, fairly frantic.

I took it for granted, as one tends to do at such times, that my peers had no problem here. Plainly these cheerful Christians must all have mastered the technique of victory over sin, and I was the only one struggling. Nowadays I take account of the way in which in tight, elitist groups everyone instinctively works to keep up appearances. At that time, however, the assured quality of others' discipleship merely awed me and drove me into further cheerless bouts of inside scraping.

And then (thank God) the group was given a library by a former member, and I was put in charge of it and found there an uncut set (twenty-three volumes) of Owen's works. Having never heard of him, and being nosey about books, I cut some pages more or less at random and dipped into the contents of this present volume. Through what I read, reinforced by another book from the library (J. C. Ryle's classic *Holiness*), my gracious God sorted me out. Like the young man I met last Sunday, I found that Owen knew exactly what was going on inside me and what I was going to think next and was reaching out across the centuries to speak to my condition.

I still think after more than five decades that Owen did more than anyone else to make me as much of a moral, spiritual, and theological realist as I have so far become. He showed me that there is far more than I had known both to indwelling sin in believers and to God's gracious work of sanctification. He searched me to the root of my being, bringing God awesomely close in the way that speakers and writers with unction are able to do. He taught me what it means to mortify sin and how to go about it. He made clear to me the real nature of the Holy Spirit's ministry in and to the believer, and of spiritual growth and progress, and of faith's victory. He told me how to understand myself as a Christian and live before God in a morally and spiritually honest way, without pretending either to be what I am not or not to be what I am. It is not too much at all to say that God used him to save my sanity. And he made every point by direct biblical exegesis, handling Scripture with a profundity that I had not met before, nor I think since save in Luther, Calvin, and Jonathan Edwards.

Many will find it hard to tune in to one who takes the holiness of God and the sinfulness of sin as seriously as Owen does, for the moral relativism and inversion of values that mark the permissive society have deeply infected the church. But that only shows how urgently we need to regain the awesome awareness of God and spiritual issues that breathes through all the work of this profoundly and biblically theocentric theologian.

—Dr. J. I. Packer

NOTES

[1] Owen, *Works* ed. W. H. Goold (London: Banner of Truth, 1966), VI.200. Note the echo of Calvin, *Institutes* I.i.I.

[2] VI.201.

[3] XVI.76.

[4] X.458.

[5] VI.213, 216.

[6] VI.254. Owen here reproduces the traditional medieval doctrine that what is *good* is also *desirable* and that objects are actually desired in virtue of the goodness, real or illusory, that appears in them.

[7] VII.397.

[8] VI.173.

[9] VI.178.

[10] VI.157.

[11] VI.181.

[12] VII.532 f.

[13] I.166 f.

[14] III.324.

[15] VI.8.

[16] VI.11.

[17] VI.192 f.

[18] VI.204 f.

[19] III.386.

[20] III.370 f., 470.

[21] III.389.

[22] III.529.

[23] III.545.

[24] *loc.cit.*

[25] III.543.

[26] On Owen's life, see Peter Toon, *God's Statesman* (Exeter: Paternoster Press, 1971).

PART I

INDWELLING SIN IN BELIEVERS

I find then a law,
that, when I would do good,
evil is present with me.
Romans 7:21

CHAPTER 1

THE NATURE OF INDWELLING SIN

men tend to think of themselves as pretty good.

Sin is within every man, no exceptions

The doctrine of indwelling sin stands out as one of the funda-mental truths of our Christian faith. The knowledge of this truth is a possession unique to those who know God and who live by divine revelation. For as "the world by wisdom knew not God," so its wise men have always ignored the inbred evil in themselves and in others (1 Cor. 1:21). *Even when it hits them, in the face men will make excuses*

Yet for Christians, the doctrine and conviction of sin form the basis of all we have to do with God—whether in pleasing Him now or enjoying Him in the hereafter. Without it, we fail to understand the mediative work of Christ, its effects, and all the benefits we enjoy from it. *Men need a mediator because of sin. no one comes to God alone!*

No wonder the doctrine of sin has been a focal subject of atten-tion by godly men, past and present. Some have focused on the nature of sin, others on the nature of its guilt, and others have traced its explanations through history. Again, others have turned attention to the remains of sin in believers, which the Scriptures talk about in so many passages. All of these aspects have been treated to the great benefit of the Church.

This study emphasizes the reality of sin's opposition to the life of grace in believers. We shall examine the effects of sin as it bankrupts some Christian lives, causing scandals and dis-graces. We also shall see how vital it is that believers should continue vigilant and diligent in faith and prayer. Thus, the call

Even the elect can suffer spiritual bankruptcy in this life. The choice is mine to be joyfully victorious or miserably defeated!

to repentance, to humility, and to self-abasement will be emphasized. Although originally composed and given to a small group, this study has been made available by God's grace to a wider audience.

[handwritten: ① Repentance ② Humility ③ self-abasement ★keys to victory?]

INDWELLING SIN IN BELIEVERS

[handwritten: sin is still an internal issue for the believer]

The great purpose of the apostle Paul in the epistle to the Romans, chapter 7, is to speak of indwelling sin in believers. Here he discusses its power, efficacy, and effects. So the apostle affirms in verse 21, "I find then a law, that, when I would do good, evil is present with me." Notice that Paul states four things in this verse. First, he says that sin is a "law." Second, he describes this discovery: "I *find* a law." Third, he indicates the context of this discovery: "when I would do good." Fourth, he specifies the state and activity of this law of sin: "evil is present with me."

[handwritten: sin is a law when I try to do good and is always present]

1. Indwelling sin is a law.

[handwritten: The law of sin: When I attempt good, evil will always be present]

By a "law" we first mean a directive rule or an *operational principle* that is effective. As a moral rule, it directs and commands, regulating the mind and will in many ways. This is what a law does. Some things it commands, and some things it forbids—with rewards and penalties—to move man to do the one and to avoid the other. *[handwritten: Like the law of gravity!]*

A secondary sense of a law is an *inward principle* that moves and inclines a person. This we call "the law of nature" when we say that everything moves toward its own end. Thus in Romans 8:2 the powerful, effective working of the Holy Spirit with the grace of Christ in the hearts of believers is called "the law of the Spirit of life." Similarly, the apostle speaks here in Romans 7:21 of indwelling sin as a "law." For it is a powerful and indwelling

[handwritten: operational principle / inward principle]

[handwritten top margin, left vertical: unbelievers do not have the law of grace w/ the Holy Spirit]

[handwritten top: Sin is by nature always working for evil! It is a force like gravity; and it hides.]

principle that inclines and forces into action what suits its own nature. So the apostle admits: "I find that this is the state of things with me, that, when I would do good, evil is present with me." We have this again in Romans 7:23 as well. *[handwritten: Sin is almost alive in its self-preservation]*

The "law," as applied to sin, has a double sense. First, it denotes the reality and nature of sins. Second, it signifies the power and efficacy of sins. Both meanings are comprised in the single term used in Romans 7:21. Thus indwelling sin is an exceedingly effective power in believers, working constantly toward evil.

Although the law of sin is (in) believers, it is not a law (to) believers. Nevertheless, even when the rule of sin is broken, its strength weakened and impaired, and its root modified, yet it is still of great force and efficacy. *When it is least felt, it is in fact most powerful.* Worldly men, in matters of spiritual and moral duties, act only according to this law and by this law. It is the ruling and prevailing principle in them affecting all moral actions with reference to a spiritual and eternal end. Our attention, however, is directed not to those in whom it has no power, but to those Christians in whom its power is more obviously discerned.

[handwritten: This is the only law to unbelievers!]

2. Believers must personally discover indwelling sin.

The apostle tells us how he has *found* this law. He has heard about such a law. It has been preached to him. This information gives him some general knowledge about it. But to experience and find it for one's self is another matter. This the apostle has personally experienced. "I have found the experience of its power and efficacy in my own life." All Christians can also likewise experience its power in themselves. Finding it for themselves, and in themselves, they can testify to the potency of its law.

[handwritten: When sin is least felt, it is in fact most powerful!!!]

I am not perfect but God has done a dramatic and miraculous work in my life!

3. Believers find this law is present in them when they "would do good." *I am not a slave to sin!*

For this law is one *unto* them, the be all and the end all of life. They would do good. Grace has sovereignty in their lives. This gives them the will to do good. They do not make it their business to always sin (see 1 John 3:9). Thus a believer does not commit sin in a habitual and willful way. Grace enables him to have a constant and usually prevailing will of doing good. While the best a non-Christian can do is to sin, the worst a Christian does is to sin. Nevertheless, the Christian finds it is when he wills to do good that "evil is present with me."

I was once lost & trapped in sin without the ability or desire to do good

4. Observe the state and activity of sin within believers.

For believers, the will to do good has two aspects. First, there is a *habitual residence* in Christians to do good. They have always an inclination to will to do good. Paul mentions this in Romans 7:18. Second, there are *special times* and *seasons* for the exercise of the principle—"when I would do good." *I desire to do what's right in God's sight.*

But sin is opposed to these two things. Sin is a contrary law to the inclination to do good. It is "when I would do good" that "evil is present with me." I know therefore when sin will appear, for it is in those times when I would do good. So Paul writes in Galatians 5:17, "For the flesh lusteth against the Spirit, and the Spirit against the flesh: and these are contrary the one to the other: so that ye cannot do the things that ye would."

In Romans 7:21 lie the dynamics of the whole course of our obedience. To be acquainted with the principles discussed above and their actions is a major part of our wisdom. Next to the reality of the free grace of God in our justification by the death of Christ, they are vital for us to experience. These are the springs of our holiness as well as of our sins, of our jobs and also of our troubles, of our refreshment and also of our sorrows.

There are actual steps you need to take. You can't dream your way to being holy!

I need to be most on guard when I desire to do good

Knowing this is to see the wisdom we need to guide and to manage our ways before God. Just as politicians must learn to know the positive and the negative aspects of government, so Christians must learn to discern what builds up and also what destroys the hearts of believers.

men need more than God or *wealth*

Men learn to know what helps their external needs—how to look after their bodies in health and in sickness and how to accumulate wealth. Yet they neglect their inward man, knowing little or nothing of the principles of God and eternity. Indeed, few labor to grow wise in such matters even though their eternal destiny depends upon it. This, therefore, must be our wisdom—a vitally necessary wisdom—if we desire to please God and to avoid that which provokes Him.

This is the most necessary skill I need to learn!

When we realize a constant enemy of the soul abides within us, what diligence and watchfulness we should have! How woeful is the sloth and negligence then of so many who live blind and asleep to this reality of sin. There is an exceeding efficacy and power in the indwelling sin of believers, for it constantly inclines itself toward evil. We need to be awake, then, if our hearts would know the ways of God.

Wake up! sloth!

Our enemy is not only *upon us*, as it was with Samson, but it is also *in us*. So if we would not dishonor God and His gospel, if we would not scandalize the saints of God, if we would not avoid our own conscience and endanger our own soul, if we would not grieve the Holy Spirit, then we must stay alert to our own danger.

The enemy is all around me + within me!

There is real loss + gain

INDWELLING SIN AS A LAW

Be ALERT!

God will not bail you out!

The danger is real!

Two general features characterize any law, including the law of sin. First, a law has *dominion*. "The law hath dominion over a man as long as he liveth" (Rom. 7:1). Literally, "it lords over a

45

man." It is properly the act of a <u>superior exacting obedience</u>. And dominion itself has a twofold aspect. It has a *moral* authority and it is *effective* in its dominion. Sin has <u>dominion over the believer</u>, though its rule is somewhat weakened.

Second, a law has *efficacy* to provoke those who offend it to do the things it requires. <u>Rewards and punishments accompany</u> a law. The <u>pleasures of sin are its rewards</u>. It threatens to deprive its adherents of its sensual contentments and to inflict temporal evils on them. Yet Moses, we are reminded, <u>chose "rather to suffer affliction with the people of God, than to enjoy the pleasures of sin for a season</u> ... for he had <u>respect unto the recompence of the reward</u>" (Heb. 11:25–26). By the miserable reward of <u>pleasure</u>, it keeps the world under obedience to it. By its <u>punishments</u>, the law of sin also keeps people subject to it.

The law of sin is not <u>a written</u>, <u>commanding law</u> so much as an <u>inbred</u>, <u>impelling</u>, <u>urging law</u>. It proposes in <u>temptation</u>, and, because it is inbred, it is strongly <u>compelling</u>. That is why God makes His new covenant <u>internal</u>, <u>implanting</u> it in the heart. In Jeremiah 31:33 God promises, "I will put my law <u>in their inward parts</u>, and write it <u>in their hearts</u>." "<u>The written law will not do</u>," He says. "I will take another course. I will turn the written law into <u>a living principle in their heart</u>. I will make it <u>an indwelling law</u>."

Likewise, the law of sin is an <u>indwelling principle</u>. It "dwelleth in me," confesses the apostle in Romans 7:20. It is "<u>present with me</u>" (7:21). It is "<u>in my members</u>" (7:23). It is an indwelling law in <u>my flesh</u>—an <u>inward habit</u> and <u>principle</u>. And its <u>power</u> is furthered by the following advantages.

- The law of sin always <u>abides</u> in the soul. It is never absent. Notice how the apostle indicates that <u>it dwells in him</u>. The law of sin is <u>not simply a visitor</u>, coming at certain times or seasons. It is at home in the soul.

46

Sin touches everything I do!

- It is always *ready* to apply itself to every end and purpose that it serves. "When I would do good," says the apostle, "evil is present with me." So you never accomplish good—when you pray, when you give alms, when you meditate, or when you do any duty to God with love for Him—without this troublesome, perplexing indweller being there to handicap you. Sin adheres as a depraved principle.

- It *applies* itself to its work with the greatest facility and ease, like "the sin which doth so easily beset us" (Heb. 12:1). It has no doors it has to open. It needs no engine by which to work. It lies in the mind and in the understanding. It is found in the will. It is in the inclinations of the affections. It is therefore so easy for it to insinuate evil in all that we do and to hinder all that is good. It has such intimacy in the soul. It possesses all those faculties of the soul whereby we must do what we do. It is always resident in the soul.

Part of fighting it is finding it.

Like cancer it mixes with all my faculties and cripples them all!

If indeed there is such a law in Christians, then it is our duty to find it out, as if a fire were in our home. Our earnestness for grace, our watchfulness, and our diligent obedience depend on this discovery. Upon this one hinge the whole course of our lives will turn. Ignorance of it breeds senselessness, carelessness, sloth, self-sufficiency, and pride—all of which the Lord's soul abhors. Eruptions into great, open, conscience-wasting, and scandalous sins are the result of a lack of due consideration of this basic law of indwelling sin.

Scandulous sin doesn't just happen it is the result of neglect.

Inquire, then, how it is with your soul. Search out its poison. When you would do good, respond in humility, self-abasement, intensity of prayer, and with diligence and watchfulness. Then you will also discover what supplies of grace and what help from the Holy Spirit will be yours.

Big sins come after little ones were ignored!

47

Attitudes
- humility
- self-abasement
- prayer
- diligence/watchfulness

Provisions
- supplies of grace
- help from the Holy Spirit

[handwritten top left: The heart should be the throne of God but sin has evaded + possessed it!]

[handwritten top right: If evil entices my heart it is because evil was within my heart to begin with.]

THE SEAT OF SIN IS IN THE HEART

[handwritten above: scripture never says sin comes from outside the heart!]

Scripture everywhere assigns the place of sin to the heart. While this should be the throne of God, sin invades and possesses it. "Madness is in their heart while they live" (Eccl. 9:3). "Out of the heart proceed evil thoughts, murders, adulteries, fornications, thefts, false witness, blasphemies" (Matt. 15:19). There are many outward temptations that beset men, exciting and stimulating them to do evil. But the root and spring of all these things lie in the heart. Temptations do not put anything into a man that is not there already.

[handwritten: Temptation has never come from outside a man!]

[handwritten left margin vertical: I am the problem!]

Hence the summary of the work and effect of this law of abiding sin is described in Genesis 6:5—"Every imagination of the thoughts of his heart was only evil continually." See Genesis 8:21 as well. So our Lord declares that "an evil man out of the evil treasure of his heart, bringeth forth that which is evil" (Luke 6:45). As a treasure it is abundant and never exhausted.

The principle applies both ways. The more a man sins, the more sin there is in him. The more good a man does by the grace of God, the more good there is in him. Both are in the heart, and no one can dispossess the evil or good.

[handwritten: Evil will always be in my heart until Glory!]

In Scripture the heart is variously used as a synonym sometimes for the *mind* and understanding, sometimes for the *will*, sometimes for the *conscience*, and sometimes for the *whole soul*. Generally, it denotes the whole soul of man and all the faculties of it. But the faculties change with the focus, so it is the mind that inquires what is good or evil and judges ethically what shall be done or refused. The affections like or dislike, cleaving to one or having aversion to another. The conscience warns and determines. All are aspects of the heart, and it is in this sense that we say the seat and subject of this law of sin is the heart of man.

Scripture links the heart with men's actions—both good and

[handwritten bottom: my affection, will, and understanding are all subject to the law of sin!]

evil—in two senses. The first sense denotes the vast *influence* of the soul on such actions. With delight, men do things heartily—that is, with their whole hearts. Even God blesses His people in love and delight "with my whole heart and with my whole soul" (Jer. 32:41). The second sense is the *resolution* and the *constancy* of the heart for such actions. As a treasure, the heart takes out constantly those things it needs or intends to use.

This then is the dwelling place of sin—the human heart. Here dwells our enemy. Within this fort the tyrant sin maintains its rebellion against God all our days. Like an enemy at war, it is not just his numbers and force of men under arms that are to be feared, but also the impregnable fortress that he possesses. Such is the heart to this enemy of God and of our souls. Let us then examine some of the features of this fortress.

In the first place the heart is *unsearchable*. "The heart is deceitful above all things, and desperately wicked: who can know it? I the LORD search the heart ..." (Jer. 17:9–10). The heart of man is known only by God. We do not know the hearts of others. We do not even know the secret intrigues and schemes, twists and turns, actions and tendencies of our own hearts. All but the infinite, all-seeing God are utterly ignorant of these things.

In the unsearchable heart resides the law of indwelling sin. Herein lies much of its security and its strength. We fight an enemy whose strength is secret and whose presence is hidden. So often when we think sin has been destroyed, it is merely out of sight. It has coverts and retreats into which we cannot pursue.

Sin lies so camouflaged—in the darkness of the mind, in the indisposition of the will, and in the worldliness of the affections—that no eye can discover it. The best of our wisdom is but to look out for its first appearances. But since nothing lies in the unsearchable heart that is not "naked and open" to God (Heb. 4:13), it is the Lord alone who penetrates to the root of things.

I can't even find the root of my problems!

My sin is smarter than me!

Not only is the heart <u>unsearchable</u>, but it is also *deceitful*. "The heart is deceitful above all things" (Jer. 17:9). There are many deceitful things in the world, whether in politics, in business, or in societies in general. But in the fraudulence of the world there is nothing that is not already in the heart. The heart itself is deceitful. So when the deceitfulness of sin is added to the heart, there is much deceitfulness indeed. Proverbs 26:25 says that "there are seven abominations in his heart." That is to say there are not only many abominations, but that there is an <u>absolutely</u> complete number—including deceitfulness.

The deceitfulness of the heart lies chiefly in two things. First, it abounds in *contradictions*, so that it <u>defies logic and consistency</u>. There are some people whose lives appear <u>contradictory.</u> They are <u>both wise and yet foolish</u>, open and yet reserved, <u>facile and yet obstinate,</u> nonvindictive and yet revengeful. So is the deceitfulness of the heart of every man, whether it be flaming hot or stone cold, weak or stubborn.

I can be wise one moment + a fool the next!

These contradictions are brought about by <u>sin, for God origi</u>nally created all things in perfect harmony and union. The mind and senses were in perfect subjection and subordination to God and His will. The will chose good, the discovery made by the mind. The affections constantly and evenly followed the understanding of the will.

But <u>the intrusion of sin has upset this harmony and orderly</u> union. So the will refuses to choose the good <u>the mind</u> discovers. The affections do not delight in what the will chooses. <u>All rebel</u> against one another. This is the result of not following God. Thus what makes the heart so <u>deceitful</u> is its <u>inconsistency</u> within itself. Its own conduct is <u>not stable.</u>

Second, the deceit of the heart lies in its many *promises* upon the first appearances of things. Sometimes the affections are touched and worked upon, and the heart disposes well. But soon

I am a walking contradiction.

I am unstable, inconsistent, and therefore deceitful!

the whole framework is changed, and all the fair promises of the heart evaporate. These false promises only promote the interest and advantages of sin. Thus God warns His people to look at their hearts lest their hearts entice and deceive them. Yet you may well ask, "Who can deal with it?"

It is not in vain, then, that the Holy Spirit exposes the heart as "deceitful above all things." The heart is uncertain in what it does, and it is false in what it promises. So we conclude with three points for application to our own hearts. *where then*

First, let us never reckon that the work of contending with our *is* own heart is ever finished. Remember the place of sin in the *hope?* heart is unsearchable. Just as many conquerors have been ruined after a victory by carelessness, so our pursuit of sin is relentless and endless. "Mortify therefore your members which are upon the earth" (Col. 3:5). Continue this as long as you live in the world. *one day I won't be on this earth!*

Second, since indwelling sin resides in various, deceitful ways, remain vigilant. An open enemy that deals only by violence always gives one some respite. When you know where to find him and what he will do next, you are free to sleep unafraid. But against adversaries that deal in treachery and deceit—having long swords reaching great distance—nothing gives security except perpetual watchfulness. It is impossible in such a situation to be too jealous, doubtful, suspicious, or watchful.

Third, then, commit the whole matter with all care and diligence to *Him who searches the heart* to the uttermost. He knows how to anticipate all its treacheries and deceit. Here is where our safety lies. This is the course of action David takes in Psalm 139. After he describes the omnipresence of God and His omniscience, he prays: "Search me, O God, and know my heart: try me, and know my thoughts" (139:23). It is as if he says, "I know very little about my own deceitful heart, even when I think I am most

This is not gentlemen's warfare, it is terrorism!

only Christ can search my heart + deliver me from temptation!

sincere. Therefore, O God, who is present in my heart, and who knows my thoughts long beforehand, undertake this work within me. Prepare it thoroughly, for You alone are able to do so."

CHAPTER 2

THE POWER OF INDWELLING SIN

We have seen the reality of indwelling sin in the heart of man as a vital principle. Let us now look further at its nature as demonstrated by its power and effectiveness. I want to emphasize the aspect of its nature that is expressed in Romans 8:7—"The carnal mind is enmity against God."

SIN IS ENMITY

There is no reconciling with sin

The only hope destruction & abolishment

The word *enmity* toward God suggests more than the hostility that enemies have toward one another. Enmity is the personification of all hostility. Enemies may be reconciled, but enmity never is reconciled. Indeed, the only way to reconcile enemies is to destroy enmity. The apostle declares, "When we were enemies, we were reconciled to God," by the atoning blood of Christ (Rom. 5:10). Thus even the greatest enemies may be reconciled. But when the apostle speaks of the principle of enmity, there is no other way to deal with it but to abolish and utterly destroy it. So he explains how Christ "abolished in His flesh the enmity" by His blood (Eph. 2:15).

If any remnant of enmity remains, it must never be tolerated to stay. Enmity may lose some of its effectiveness, but—like every single drop of poison—it will infest and spread its poison again. Or like a spark of fire, it will still go on burning. So the apostle,

You can't tolerate sin!

Sin will always be emnity towards God

knowing its character, cries out in Romans 7:24 for a total deliverance from its power: "Who shall deliver me from the body of this death?" Mortification abates its *force*, but it cannot deal with its *nature*. Grace changes the nature of man, but nothing changes the nature of sin.

"God is love," we read in 1 John 4:8. God is eternally excellent and desirable above all. He is so in Himself, He is so in the death of His Son, and in all the inexpressible fruits of it (by which we are what we are and in which all our future hopes depend). Yet it is against this God that we may carry an enmity all our lives. It is an enmity incapable of cure or reconciliation. Our only salvation is enmity's destruction.

As we have said, it is possible for enemies to be reconciled, as David was with Saul. The course he took we may all take—by finding out what provokes our enemy and by removing it to make peace. In 1 Samuel 26:19 David says, "If the LORD have stirred thee up against me, let him accept an offering: but if they be the children of men, cursed be they before the LORD." Whether the offer of reconciliation comes from God or from men, it brings the hope of peace. But when a man deals with enmity itself, we can expect nothing but continued fighting until one party is eventually destroyed. For if enmity is not overcome and destroyed, it will overcome and destroy the soul.

I am losing!

Here then is where much of the power of sin lies. Its enmity admits no terms of peace. There may be a truce where there is no peace. But with this enemy we can have neither truce nor peace. So it is vain to hope for any reconciliation with sin. Some try, making "provision for the flesh, to fulfil the lusts thereof" (Rom. 13:14). But it is like trying to put a fire out with wood and oil. It merely adds fuel to the fire and so increases it. The only way to deal with a fire in your home is to put it out. Nothing else will

I am fighting emnity itself there is no reconcilliation!

This is a fight to the death!

do. Since the very nature of sin is enmity, the only relief one can find is to utterly destroy it.

SIN IS ENMITY TOWARD GOD

Sin fights to destroy God

Not only is sin enmity itself, but it is "enmity against God." Indeed, it has chosen to have God Himself as its almighty enemy. In various passages of Scripture, sin is spoken of as *our* enemy. So 1 Peter 2:11 says: "Abstain from fleshly lusts, which war against the soul." Again it is said, "The flesh lusteth against the Spirit" (Gal. 5:17). Sin fights the spiritual principle that is in us. It fights to destroy our soul. Although it opposes the work of grace in us, its nature and purpose above all is to oppose God. *Sin is God's enemy, its what killed christ!*

When we think of God as the lawgiver, of God as holy, of God as the author of salvation, then we see how deadly serious is the enmity of sin. Why does sin oppose duty, so that the good we would do, we do not do? Why does sin make the soul carnal, indisposed, unbelieving, unspiritual, weary, and wandering? Simply because it is enmity to God with whom the soul aims to have communion.

Sin has a command of Satan rather like that issued to the Assyrians by their king: "Fight neither with small nor great, save only with the king of Israel" (1 Kings 22:31). Sin is not opposed to small or great so much as against God Himself. It is like the Assyrians who pursued Jehoshaphat, thinking he was Ahab the king. When they discovered he was not the king of Israel, they ceased the pursuit. In the same way, Satan only attracts those who live in God's presence. The rest are left alone, for the enmity lies primarily against God. *I have a target on my back*

Another aspect of enmity is this: Sin attacks holiness and God's authority in our lives. It hates the yoke of the Lord.

How do I win against such 55 hostility!?

[handwritten: Sin is violence against God against]

"Thou hast been weary of me," says God to sinners during their performance of various duties (Isa. 43:22). Indeed, every act of sin is the fruit of being weary against God. At the bottom of our hearts, the nature of sin is to "say unto God, Depart from us" (Job 21:14; 22:17). It is to oppose God, to rebel, to cast off His yoke, and to destroy the dependence every creature has upon the Creator.

In Romans 8:7 the apostle gives the reason why "the carnal mind is enmity against God." It is "because it is not subject to the will of God, nor can it be." It never is, it never will, nor can it ever be subject to God. Its whole nature consists of opposition to God, and it never will be anything else.

[handwritten: Sin is opposition to God, opposition?]

THE ENMITY OF SIN AS UNIVERSAL AND ABSOLUTE

Moreover, enmity to God is absolute and universal in its extent, for this enmity is intrinsic within sin. Such enmity is universal to all of God, it is universal to the soul, and it is absolutely so in all of its operations.

1. Sin is universal in its enmity toward God.

If there were some attribute or act of God that was not enmity to sin, the soul of man could find shelter there. But there is none, for enmity lies against all of God and everything wherein or whereby we relate to God. Sin is enmity to God as God, and therefore to all of God—whether it is God's goodness, His holiness, His mercy, His grace, or His promises. There is nothing of God that it is not implacably against.

Likewise, there is no duty we perform for God that sin does not oppose. And the more spirituality or holiness there is in what we do, the greater is its enmity to it. Thus those who seek most for God experience the strongest opposition.

[handwritten: I am facing very little opposition right now!]

[handwritten: How do I win?]

[handwritten margin note: There is no haven from sin! Every inch must be fought for!]

2. Sin is universal in its enmity against the soul.

If only sin had been content with subduing one faculty of the soul or leaving one affection that was free of its yoke! Then it might have been possible to oppose or subdue it. But when Christ Himself comes as Conqueror to visit the soul, He finds no resting place. He must fight for every inch of territory—within the mind, within the affections, within the will. No area of one's life indeed is secured without struggle. Even when God's grace enters the soul of man, sin is still there, and pervasively so.

Thus we find there is universal warfare in the soul of man. The mind contends with its own darkness and vanity. The will wrestles with its own stubbornness, obstinacy, and perversity. Every affection deals with its own willfulness, sensuality, and aversion of God. Thus our knowledge is imperfect, our obedience is weak, our love is mixed in its virtues, our fear of the Lord is not pure, and our delight in God is not free and noble.

3. Sin is constant in its power of enmity.

[handwritten margin note: I line up against a 300 pnd lineman everyday!]

Sin never wavers, yields, or gives up in spite of all the powerful opposition it encounters from the law of the gospel. If we only believed this, we would be less careless in carrying around that implacable enmity with us. It is well that those who are vigilant should weaken its force within them. But how sad is the deception of those who deceive themselves into thinking they have no sin (see 1 John 1:8). *only few succeed!*

Sin Is Aversion of God

The actions and operations of sin are twofold: first by aversion and second by opposition. These two elements help us to see the operation of enmity within us against God. *Aversion* is when two parties loathe each other. The prophet writes, "My soul loathed them, and their soul also abhorred me" (Zech. 11:8). It is a mutual enmity, such as the Jews and the Samaritans had for each other (see John 4:9). *Opposition* or contention is another product of enmity. As Isaiah 63:10 says, "He was turned to be their enemy, and he fought against them." This speaks of how God turned away from His people. So both of these are the effects of enmity.

The hostility will never end! The only answer is to have greater hostility with me!

Sin is first of all aversion of God. Sin is indisposed to duty whereby communion with God is obtained. All weariness of duty, all carnality, and all formality in duty spring from this root. So we are warned: "Keep thy foot when thou goest to the house of God" (Eccl. 5:1). In other words, God is saying, "Do you have any spiritual duty to perform? Do you propose to seek communion with God? Look then to yourself, to take care of the inclinations of your heart, for they will wander and be deflected by aversion to what you propose."

Aversion will misdirect us whenever we seek to do good. "When I would do good, evil is present with me" (Rom. 7:21). Paul is saying, "Whenever I have spiritual desires for good, sin is present to hinder and to obstruct me in my duty." This is because sin abhors and loathes whatever we would do for God. Sin allows an outward, bodily appearance of worship of God; with that it is not concerned, for sin keeps the heart far away (see Ezek. 33:31).

Some people believe they have such freedom and liberty from sin that this aversion is not within themselves. But I fear this pseudofreedom turns out to be the result of one or two causes. For many it is ignorance of the true condition and state of their own souls. Like the Pharisees, they are in the dark about themselves. That is why they boast of what they do for God. Then some are without a personal relationship to Jesus Christ and have no real communion with Him. So whatever

Sin will never change! I must change! Adapt! evolve!

duties of obedience they perform, they have little or no opposition from sin.

Very different is the aversion of sin to those who seek only God in their lives. First, these believers often experience this aversion of sin to God within their *affections*. A secret, deep conflict in relating to God resides in them, unless the hand of God in His Spirit is high and strong upon their soul. Even when convictions, a sense of duty, and true esteem of and communion with God have all carried the soul into the closet of prayer, yet there may still be a resistant loathing to pray. Yes, it may even be a strong opposition to prayer, so that the soul catches on to any excuse or diversion it can embrace, knowing it will be wounded in spirit by neglecting prayer.

A second source of aversion to God is discovered in the *mind*. Job speaks of the ease with which we will fill our mouths with arguments before God (see Job 23:4). We experience times also when our mind—clearly knowing the duties we should perform before God—only wanders and flags listlessly, all from the secret aversion of indwelling sin toward God. This is why some complain that they are unable to meditate.

Aversion is also found in the *practical duties* we need to perform. The difficulties raised against these duties, the lack of consistency in doing them, their neglect, and the lack of continuation in the faith (eventually leading to apostasy) all are evidence of indwelling sin. Satan blinds people to strive to serve God without having a real relationship to Him. To let sin alone in our lives is to permit sin to grow until it chokes and blinds the conscience. Not to conquer sin is to be conquered by sin.

What is done in private is also found in *public duties*. How we have to struggle and strive in them, especially against the spirituality of such duties! The mind and the affections are mixed in their motives, sometimes giving evidence of the ugly, nasty

Christ is powerful more powerful than sin!

reality of sin. Indeed, let a man unclothe any duty, whether private or public, of the false report it gains outwardly (rendering the duty unfit for God). Then he will assuredly feel the power and the effects of sin's aversions to God.

How then shall we keep the soul from sin's aversions, so that we may have a holy frame of mind and spirit? Five means may be outlined.

Obedience in all areas!

1. Have a disposition of heart fixed upon God.

Only a holy frame or disposition will enable us to say with the psalmist, "My heart is fixed, O God, my heart is fixed" (Ps. 57:7). It is utterly impossible to keep the heart in a holy frame in any one duty, unless it is also so in all duties before God. If sin entangles us in one area of our life, it will ensnare every area of our life. A contented, even disposition and spirit in all duties and in all ways is the only preservative.

Consistency must be maintained in our private and public duties, for there is a harmony in obedience. If you break one part, you interrupt the whole. Thus David says, "Then shall I not be ashamed, when I have respect unto all thy commandments" (Ps. 119:6). A universal respect for all of God's commandments is the only preservative against shame.

2. Labor to prevent the beginnings of the workings of this aversion.

Let grace proceed before every duty. "Watch unto prayer" anticipating danger in every duty (1 Peter 4:7). Look out then for all temptations, for if they are not dealt with in the incipient encounter, they will prevail later. Prevent sin from negotiating with the soul. Peter had no sooner said, "Be it far from thee, Lord," than Jesus immediately replied, "Get thee behind me, Satan" (Matt. 16:22–23). Similarly, we ought to say, "Get behind me, law of sin. Depart!"

60

I have to fight for every inch of holiness

3. Although sin does its work, never allow it to make a conquest.

Do not grow weary because of its tenacity or faint because of its opposition. As the apostle exhorts, "We desire that every one of you do shew the same diligence to the full assurance of hope unto the end: That ye be not slothful" (Heb. 6:11–12). Hold out, and do not be diverted by the power of temptation, by discouragement, and above all, by the insensitivity to the aversion of sin toward God.

Our Lord enjoins, "Men ought always to pray, and not to faint" (Luke 18:1). Opposition will arise, and none so keen as from our own hearts. Take heed "lest you be wearied," says the apostle, "and faint in your minds" (Heb. 12:3). The same caution is given in Romans 12:12— "Rejoicing in hope; patient in tribulation; continuing instant in prayer"—and again in Romans 6:12, where we read, "Let not sin therefore reign in your mortal body, that ye should obey it in the lusts thereof." Yield not then, but hold out in conflict. *hold on! charge!*

Wait on God and you shall prevail. We have this promise in Isaiah 40:31—"They that wait upon the LORD shall renew their strength; they shall mount up with wings as eagles; they shall run, and not be weary; and they shall walk, and not faint." What is difficult to do now will increase in difficulty, if we give way to it now. But if we stand fast now, God promises we shall prevail later. *renewed strength! Flight! run!*

4. Carry always with you a constant, humbling sense of the aversion sin has within our nature to true spirituality.

After discovering all the kindness we have received by God's grace, surely all we can do is to walk closely with Him. Is not our fruitfulness from Him? Is not our light from Him? Have we not

He that is in me is mightier than He that is in the world!!!

gained all by drawing near to Him? Have we not obtained all rest and peace from Him? Is He not the fountain and spring of all mercies and other desirable things? Have we not received from Him more than our heart could conceive or our tongue express?

If these things are so, why then should we harbor a cursed dislike of Him and His ways in our foolish and wretched hearts? We should be ashamed of this aversion. If God delights to dwell in a humble and contrite spirit, let us walk in a humbling sense of His presence. This will weaken the evil of indwelling sin.

5. Finally, let us labor to possess this mind with the beauty and excellency of spiritual things.

[margin note: Fight fire with fire]

[margin note: Replace the pleasures of sin w/ the delights of God]

Cherish these things as desirable and lovely to the soul. It is an innate principle that the soul will not continue worshiping God if it is not discovering the beauty and comeliness of such worship. So when men lose all spiritual sense and savor of the things of God, they will invent substitutes—outward purposes and gorgeous forms of worship using images, pictures, and other such things.

Unless men see a beauty and delight in the worship of God, they will act averse to it. See God then as the eternal spring of all beauty. Love Christ as the hope of all nations. Admire the Holy Spirit as the great beautifier of souls. To acquaint the soul with these divine attractions is to weaken the aversion indwelling sin has within us to the things of God.

[margin note: God is the source of all beauty]

SIN IS OPPOSITION TO GOD

Sin is enmity to God, then, by aversion. But it is also opposition to God by its contention, as light to darkness, heat to cold, virtue to vice, or sin to grace. "These are contrary the one to the other" (Gal. 5:17).

There are four ways in which this opposition of sin toward

[handwritten: The only way to deal with sin is to oppose it!]

[handwritten: This is the nature of life!]

God is seen. First, it is seen by sin's general inclination to lust *[handwritten: opposite]* (see Gal. 5:17). Second, it is seen by its warfare (see Rom. 7:23; James 4:1; 1 Peter 2:11). Third, it is seen by the way it captures the soul (see Rom. 7:23). Fourth, it is seen by the way it grows and grows, ultimately generating madness (see Eccl. 9:3).

1. Sin opposes God by lust.

Hence all the actions of sin are called "the lust of the flesh" (Gal. 5:16). "Make not provision for the flesh," the apostle warns, "to fulfil the lusts thereof" (Rom. 13:14). The mind as well as the flesh lusts. Sin opposes God by this lust in two ways.

First, *the heart has a hidden propensity to do evil.* The heart habitually waits to do evil in us. Under the dominion of sin, it is said of man, "every imagination of the thoughts of his heart was only evil continually" (Gen. 6:5). It fashions only what is evil. The law of sin is absolutely predominant in this way. It is like poison in the bloodstream that has no antidote to allay its virulence. Here a distinction should be made, however, between the habitual frame of the heart we all have and the inclinations of the heart that may be changed by the grace of God.

Concerning the former, Paul confesses, "Evil is present with me" (Rom. 7:21). It is always there, lusting to sin. It is a river full of hidden springs that enable it to continually flow. If the springs dry up, however, the water level will abate. In vain, men dam this river in their attempt to contain it with their convictions, resolutions, vows, and promises. They may check it for a time, but when the springs rise again, the water will flood once more.

This habitual propensity to sin is discovered in two ways. First, in its unexpected eruptions into the soul by foolish or sinful imaginations, we discover wicked thoughts we never knew we had. So Paul cautions us to be vigilant lest we be surprised and "overtaken in a fault" (Gal. 6:1).

[handwritten: This is all there is to life = war, opposition, strife, fighting]

Vanity! All is Vanity!

On the other hand, we may be doing something good, and sin suddenly enters our consciousness to entice us unexpectedly. How much communion with God is spoiled in this way. How often meditations are interrupted, defiling the mind and conscience. I know of no greater burden in the life of a believer than these involuntary invasions of sin within the soul.

These invasions of sin appear to be involuntary because they lack the consent of the will. Yet it is the corruption of the will that is the source of those incursions of evil within our consciousness. For this reason the apostle cries out, "Who shall deliver me from the body of this death?" (Rom. 7:24).

But as we have noted, *the heart also has inclinations to do evil* that may be changed by God's grace. Just as the heart inclines itself toward evil, so it can be inclined to resist evil if we are believers. Our Savior says of the assaults and temptations of Satan, "The prince of this world cometh, and hath nothing in me" (John 14:30). Christ had more temptations than any of the sons of men, yet He dealt only with that which was without. His heart was always pure from evil inclinations.

Lust consents in its actual contact and is pressing in upon that which is evil. It lusts and continually lusts in a chain reaction of lust upon lust. So James 1:14 tells us, "Every man is tempted, when he is drawn away of his own lust, and enticed." If we keep our hearts pure, however, the temptations that come from without will have no power over us. So the power of sin is to beget sin, warns the apostle. We are to keep ourselves from every figment of an idea of evil within our hearts (see 1 Thess. 5:22). Then we will be kept from lusting.

2. Sin opposes God by warfare.

Sin stirs up men's minds to have an appetite and inclination toward lusting and more lusting. But it cannot rest there, for it *win the battles to win the war! Every inch matters!*

then proceeds to <u>fight</u> and <u>contend with vigor</u> to obtain its <u>end</u> and <u>purpose.</u> Much sin could be avoided if only lust did not contend in this way. But <u>it pursues its objective vigorously and relentlessly in open conflict.</u> By this means, <u>wicked men enflame themselves, setting sparks into flames</u> (see Isa. 57:5).

Now the warfare of sin consists of three things: <u>its rebellion against grace</u>; <u>its assault of the soul</u>, <u>contending for the rule and sovereignty over it</u>; and its <u>entangling of the affections.</u>

"<u>I see another law in my members</u>," says the apostle in Romans 7:23, "<u>warring against the law of my mind.</u>" There are, it seems, two laws within us: the <u>law of sin</u> and the <u>law of grace.</u> But <u>contrary laws cannot both obtain sovereign power over the same person at the same time.</u> The <u>sovereign power in believers is in the hand of the law of grace.</u> This is what the apostle declares: "<u>I delight in the law of God in the inward man</u>" (Rom. 7:22). Obedience to this law is performed with (delight and peace) in the inward man, because its authority is <u>lawful and good.</u> But <u>when rebellion against the law of grace takes place by the power of sin,</u> then there is <u>conflict and war</u> (see Rom. 7:15–16).

But is it not strange that the law of grace not only <u>prevails</u> in the <u>affections</u> (see Rom. 7:22), but also in the <u>will</u> (7:18), and in the <u>understanding</u> (7:15–16)? Yet how is it then that the law of grace—though it is <u>gladly</u> and <u>freely accepted by the soul—is not fully sovereign in the life of the believer?</u> The apostle admits, "<u>How to perform that which is good I find not</u>" (Rom. 7:18). The opposition sin creates to the general disposition of the soul gives us our answer.

Because of the opposition of sin to the general purpose of the soul, <u>no one walks in perfect conformity to God's will in all things.</u> Clearly, it is God's purpose for man to do so. Cleaving to the Lord with purpose of heart is <u>the disposition of the upright</u> (see Acts 11:23).

＊ Life is lived in seconds!

＊ take care of the seconds & the hours, days, years will take care of themselves !!!

But Paul confesses, "Not as though I had already attained, either were already perfect: but I follow after, if that I may apprehend that for which also I am apprehended of Christ Jesus. Brethren, I count not myself to have apprehended: but this one thing I do, forgetting those things which are behind, and reaching forth unto those things which are before, I press toward the mark for the prize of the high calling of God in Christ Jesus" (Phil. 3:12–14).

Notice how Paul uses three words to indicate the vigor, the earnestness, the diligence, and the constancy that are needed in this pursuit of purpose: "I follow after," "I reach forward," and "I press toward the mark." These are needed because, without them, the heart is seduced into rebellion by the law of sin.

Notice how sin assaults the soul in deliberate attacks. Peter warns us: "Abstain from fleshly lusts, which war against the soul" (1 Peter 2:11). "From whence come wars and fightings among you?" James asks. "Come they not hence, even of your lusts that war in your members?" (James 4:1). Sin often assaults by the vanity of the mind, or by the sensuality of the affections, or by the folly of the imagination. Hence the apostle cries out in Romans 7:24, "Who shall deliver me from the body of this death?"

In the distress of helplessness, there is nothing more marvelous, and yet nothing more dreadful, than the importunity of the soul before the realities of sin. The soul does not know what to do. It hates, abhors, and abominates the evil toward which it tends. The soul despises its thoughts, and yet they impose upon it. Why then do they so dominate him? "Alas," Paul says, "it is no more I that do it, but sin that dwelleth in me" (Rom. 7:17). Paul is saying, "I have a ruthless enemy inside me, whom I cannot get rid of. O wretched man that I am! Who shall deliver me?"

Sin also carries on its war by entangling the affections and *more cold, + violent*

drawing them into an alliance against the mind. Grace may be enthroned in the mind, but if sin controls the affections, it has seized a fort from which it will continually assault the soul. Hence, as we shall see, mortification is chiefly directed to take place upon the affections.

In Colossians 3:5 we have the command, "Mortify therefore your members which are upon the earth; fornication, unclean-ness, inordinate affection, evil concupiscence, and covetousness, which is idolatry." The members that are upon the earth are the affections or inclinations of heart. This becomes the principal seat of sin in the believer. Every day we see prominent Christians that have visibly unmortified hearts and lifestyles. Clearly their affections have not been "crucified with Christ" (Gal. 2:20).

Affections = Normandy!

In this spiritual warfare, the Christian needs to be taught to walk humbly before God. Two things are needed to humble us. First, let us consider God in His greatness, glory, holiness, power, majesty, and authority. Then, let us consider ourselves in our mean, abject, and sinful condition—especially in our enmity against God, which still remains in our hearts. It is clear evidence of a gracious soul when it willingly dives into the secret part of its own heart and rips open whatever evil and corruption lie there.

The prophet says of Ephraim, he "loveth to tread out the corn" (see Hos. 10:11). In the same way, most men love to hear the doc-trine of grace, of pardon from sin, of unmerited love. But to break up the "fallow ground" of the hearts, to weed out the grass and thorns growing there, is not a task anyone delights in doing (Hos. 10:12). Yet it is sloth and neglect that we need to shake off; otherwise, we shall deceive ourselves.

To break up this fallow ground, as we have said, we must first walk with God. His delight is with the humble and contrite, with

humble yourself in the sight of the Lord and He will lift you up!

those who tremble at His word. It is the condition of those who have a due sense of their unworthiness. This begets reverence of God, a sense of our distance from Him, admiration of His grace and condescension, and a deep awareness of His mercy.

Then in walking with others, we are kept from the great evil of judging them without mercy and censoring them with harshness. This leads us to meekness and compassion, as well as to readiness to forgive and to pass over the offenses of others. We are to consider what our own state is (see Gal. 6:1).

The person who understands the evil in his own heart is the only person who is useful, fruitful, and solid in his beliefs and obedience. Others only delude themselves and thus upset families, churches, and all other relationships. In their self-pride and judgment of others, they are showing great inconsistency.

3. Sin also opposes God by leading the soul captive.

"I see another law," Paul writes, "bringing me into captivity to the law of sin" (Rom. 7:23). Here the apostle is emphasizing not only the power and actions of the law of sin, but its success. No one aims at greater success than to lead their enemies captive, so Scripture uses this as a figure of great success. Thus the Lord Christ, in His victory over Satan, is said to have "led captivity captive" (Eph. 4:8).

This captivity is to "the law of sin"—not to this or that particular sin, but to the basic principle of sinning. That is why David prayed so earnestly, "Cleanse thou me from secret faults. Keep back thy servant also from presumptuous sins; let them not have dominion over me: then shall I be upright" (Ps. 19:12–13). "This is my condition," he argues. "Restrain me from those sins, such as pride and overconfidence, that make a captive of me." Likewise, Jabez prays, "Oh that thou wouldest bless me indeed, and enlarge my coast, and that thine hand might be with me, and that thou wouldest keep me from evil, that it may not grieve me!" (1 Chron. 4:10).

When men fall into sin, they are also held captive by it. Paul speaks of those who "may recover themselves out of the snare of the devil, who are taken captive by him at his will" (2 Tim. 2:26). Although it appears that their own lust deceives them, they are actually brought into bondage by Satan's snare. So it says they are "taken alive," as if they were trapped animals.

We may well ask this question: Is the prevailing power of a particular sin found in the sin itself, or does it derive its energy from the influence of temptation over it? This may be answered in two ways.

First, much of the prevalence of sin is from Satan himself when a particular sin has no advantage or attraction to us. If it is not something toward which we are naturally inclined, then we may attribute its power directly to Satan, who imposes his suggestions on the imagination.

Likewise, when a dominant lust has no direct appeal to the flesh, its attraction is also from Satan. Usually, lust appeals to the flesh by the allurement of profits and pleasures. When this is not so, then Satan again is the source of it.

Thus, when Paul speaks in Romans 7 of our captivity, not to this or that particular sin, but to the law of sin—whose presence and burden we are forced to bear, whether we like it or not—then we are forced to sigh and cry out for deliverance. The idea of captivity suggests a condition we do not wish to experience. We are opposed to it. But it is forced upon us against our will, which the spiritual habit of grace would help us resist.

We may observe four things, then, about the captivity to sin. First, *the power of sin is great* to bring us into such slavery. Second, *sin makes many particular successes* to lead men captive. There are also many stages of servitude into which a man may be brought deeper and deeper. Third, *captivity is a miserable and wretched condition* to be in. When one is forced into a situation that one loathes, then the yoke rubs hard against the neck. It even breaks the heart. Fourth, *captivity is a condition particular to Christians.* Unregenerate men are never held captive by the law of sin. They are captured by this or that particular sin. But this is the captivity of believers who do not will to sin. Instead, they really want to love God and to hate sin.

Only christians struggle to be free!

4. Sin generates madness.

The law of sin has yet another feature. It generates rage and madness. It makes a man like a "wild ass" (Jer. 2:24; Hos. 8:9). It makes idolaters, enraged with their lust, "mad upon their idols" (Jer. 50:38). *Sin is insanity*

The nature of the law of sin is to tear and to torment the soul in plain madness of lust. This may occur with some great temptation, as David had with Bathsheba. The burning embers are blown up by Satan's bellows into a fiery furnace. Likewise, a former experience of sin is an advantage Satan uses to make another, more spectacular assault. Without the previous entry of sin, the greater assault is not possible.

The rage and madness of sin lead to the rejection of the rule of force, even though it is only momentary rejection. The present sense of Christ is then lost. This happens when the inclinations of the affections toward Christ are weakened, clouded, or stifled in some way. Disobedience then ensues, in spite of the warning, "Do not this abominable thing that I hate" (Jer. 44:4).

Such madness is often accompanied by recklessness and fearlessness. The power of consistent judgment is swept aside along with all the influence it exerts. This leads men to despising God and His ways—even if it means damnation—as long as their lusts are satisfied.

Sin clouds out the Son

momentary insanity

oh Lord hedge me in!

YET GOD DEALS WITH INDWELLING SIN

The fear of God is the beginning of wisdom

However, even when the soul has broken away from the power of renewing grace, God deals with it by preventing grace. This is illustrated in Hosea 2:6, where God says: "Therefore, behold, I will hedge up thy way with thorns, and make a wall, that she shall not find her paths." God sets up barriers to obstruct the path to sins. He does this in two ways.

First, God does so by presenting us with *rational considerations.* These considerations are the fear of death, of judgment, and of hell. We should fear to fall into the hands of the living God, for He is a "consuming fire" (Heb. 12:29). As long as a man is under the rule of the Spirit of life, the love of Christ constrains him (see 2 Cor. 5:14). The principle of his doing good and abstaining from evil is faith working by love.

If this blessed yoke is cast aside for a season, God may then set up a hedge of terror before the soul reminding it of death and judgment to come. He fills the soul with the considerations of all the evil consequences of sin to deter it from its purpose. God also reminds the soul of all the temporal consequences of sin—shame, reproach, and punishment. By these means God sets a hedge before us.

Second, God uses *providential events* for the same purpose. These may be positive or negative in character. Positively, God causes the soul to desist from sin—and its lustful pursuit—by affliction. He chastens men with bodily sickness, to turn them from their purpose, and to hide sin from them (see Job 33:17–19). God sometimes visits them with adverse circumstances to their reputation, their relationships, their fortunes, and to other desirable things. Finally, He showers and heaps such mercies upon them that they realize once more from Whom these blessings come and yet against Whom they are rebelling.

Negatively, God may actually hinder some from their pursuit of sin. This we shall consider later.

Yet in spite of this, the rage and madness of sin may continue unabated. Sin does this by the possession of the mind, suppressing any reflection on the consequences of its actions. Sin also does so by the secret, stubborn resolve to venture forward on its mad course, whatever the consequences. In this way we see the force, strength, and violence of sin in all its naked power.

CHAPTER 3

THE DECEIT OF INDWELLING SIN

We have seen that sin is powerful. It is also deceitful. The apostle gives this warning in Hebrews 3:13—"Take heed that you are not hardened by the deceitfulness of sin." Because of this deceitfulness of sin, the heart that harbors sin is said to be "deceitful above all things" (Jer. 17:9).

In some matters a man may be very competent. But this is not so with respect to sin. "For vain man would be wise, though man be born like a wild ass's colt"—a poor, empty nothing (Job 11:12). On account of this law of sin, "they are wise to do evil, but to do good they have no knowledge" (Jer. 4:22).

Likewise, the apostle says, "The old man ... is corrupt according to the deceitful lusts" (Eph. 4:22). Every lust is deceitful—not inherently so, but because of what is communicated to it by this law of sin. It is as polluted as water from a contaminated spring. Thus the "man of sin" will come in and with "the deception of unrighteousness" (2 Thess. 2:10).

Now people do not desire unrighteousness as a reputation because it is decried in society. But the deception of sin stays concealed and less obvious. The apostle speaks of those under the power of sin as "deceived" (Titus 3:3). The life of evil men consists of nothing but "deceiving, and being deceived" (2 Tim. 3:13). This is also the character of our enemy. He is deceitful. Against such a one no security exists but vigilance.

sin is by nature deceitful

It deceives the sinner who is trying to deceive others

Sin begets deceit and deceit begets sin

SIN'S DECEPTION OF THE MIND

Deception & sin go hand in hand

Scripture also emphasizes that deceit is most often the origin of sinning. Sin proceeds only when deception goes before it (see 1 Tim. 2:13–14). The apostle argues that Adam (though first formed) was not first in transgression because he was not first deceived. Eve, though created later, was first in being deceived and then first in sin. Thus even the first sin began in deceit, as Eve says: "The serpent beguiled me, and I did eat" (Gen. 3:13). She thought to extenuate her guilt by blaming the serpent, but in fact she only added to her sin. Thus the apostle also shows that deceit and transgression go hand in hand.

Satan deals in the economy of deceit

"The same method of corruption," he says, "continues as it did in the beginning: beguiling (or deceiving) goes before, and sin (the actual accomplishment of it) follows after" (2 Cor. 11:3). Thus all the great works that Satan does in this world—in stirrng up men to oppose the Lord Jesus Christ—he does by deceit. He is "the Devil, and Satan, which deceiveth the whole world" (Rev. 12:9; see 20:10).

No wonder so many warnings abound in Scripture, cautioning us to take heed lest we become deceived and fall into sin (see Luke 21:8; 1 Cor. 6:9; 15:33; Gal. 6:7; Eph. 5:6). From these and other testimonies we can learn how deceit leads to sin.

Lust is for the affections; Deceit is for the mind

The basis for the efficacy of deceit is its effect upon the mind. For sin deceives the mind. When sin attempts to enter into the soul by some other way (such as by the affections), the mind checks and controls it. But when deceit influences the mind, the chance of sinning multiplies.

The mind is the leading faculty of the soul. When the mind fixes upon an object or course of action, the will and the affections follow suit. They are incapable of any other consideration. Thus, while the entanglement of the affections in sin is often very

Above all guide your mind! (handwritten)

troublesome, it is the deceit of the mind that is always t
dangerous situation because of its role in all other operations or
the soul. The mind's office is to guide, to direct, to choose, and to
lead. "If therefore the light that is in us be darkness, how great is
that darkness!" (Matt. 6:23).

We also see the danger of sin's deception of the mind by exam-
ining the general nature of deceit. It consists in falsely presenting
things to the mind in such a way that their true nature, causes,
effects, or present conditions to the soul remain hidden. Thus
deceit conceals what should be exposed, whether it be circumstances or consequences.

Sin grows in darkness as mold grows in moisture (handwritten)

Just as Satan deceived our first parents, he continues to do so
today by misrepresentation. The fruit was desirable; that was
obvious to the eye. Satan then secretly suggested that God
sought to limit their happiness by forbidding them to eat it. But
Satan hid from them the fact that this was a test of their obedience and that certain if not immediate ruin would ensue if they
disobeyed God. Satan deceived them by simply proposing
immediate gratification, which the fruit certainly provided. This
is the nature of deceit. By only presenting the desirable aspects
of temptation, it deceives the mind into making a false judgment.
Jacob used deception in this way to receive the blessing from
Isaac that rightly belonged to his brother Esau (see Gen. 27).

Deceit also operates slowly, little by little, so that its
manipulation is not exposed all at once. In the story of the Fall,
Satan acts in a sequence of steps. First, he removes the objection
of death. Next, he offers them great knowledge. Then he suggests that they will become as gods. Each step hides aspects of
reality and only presents half-truths.

Likewise, Stephen describes Pharaoh as having dealt deceit-
fully with the Israelites (see Acts 7:19). Exodus chapter 1 tells us
how he did this. "Come, let us deal wisely," he says as he begins

(left margin, handwritten) "Bacteria does not grow on sterile instruments!" "Sin does not grow in light of exposure."

to oppress them (1:10). Having enslaved them, he then proceeds to slaughter their infants. Thus Pharaoh fell upon the Israelites gradually. This, too, is how sin proceeds in the soul.

The apostle sums this up when he says, "Every man is tempted, when he is drawn away of his own lust, and enticed. Then when lust hath conceived, it bringeth forth sin: and sin, when it is finished, bringeth forth death" (James 1:14–15). Just as our first parents were deceived, the old enemy slowly deceives us in the same way. When we sin, we also tend to blame everything else, and if this fails, we even blame God. Thus the apostle rebukes, "Let no man say when he is tempted, I am tempted of God: for God cannot be tempted with evil, neither does He tempt any man" (James 1:13). The whole guilt lies with the sinner, and therefore the whole punishment will yet fall upon him.

The ultimate purpose of sin is to bring death. "Sin, when it is finished, bringeth forth death" (James 1:15). But it hides this by confusing the sinner. Sin never admits its purpose is so deadly, so it has to deceive.

Sin deceives chiefly by temptation. "Every man is tempted … of his own lust" (James 1:14). I do not intend to speak primarily on temptation, for I have done so in another treatise [see Part II]. It is enough to note here that the life of temptation lies in deceit. It is the business of sin to tempt or to deceive; they are the same thing. This we have seen in the story of the fall: "The serpent beguiled me" (Gen. 3:13). This beguiling occurs by one's own lust or indwelling sin, which we have already seen are the same thing.

Sin proceeds in temptation step by step, for it is inherent in sin to gradually advance to its own advantage. Five steps may be distinguished in James 1:14–15.

First, sin deceives: "Every man is tempted, when he is drawn away by his own lust."

Second, sin entices: "and is enticed."

Third, sin conceives: "Then when lust hath conceived."

Fourth, sin develops: "it bringeth forth sin" (as children are conceived by fornication).

Fifth, sin finishes: "Sin, when it is finished, bringeth forth death." (The real conception of sin is not just the conception of children by lust; it is *death* that it really conceives. This is its deadly end.)

Our attention focuses on the first three major steps of sin in temptation in this chapter and the next. Since we are concerned about believers, God in His mercy keeps us from the last two consequences.

Sin draws us away from God, diverting us from the path of holiness and obedience. Now the deceit of sin operates upon the mind. As the discerning, judging, and determining faculty, the mind acts as the eyes of the soul. Without its guidance, we would wander like the Israelites in the wilderness of this world. So sin aims first of all to distract and to divert the mind from the discharge of its duty.

The duty of the mind consists of two things. God requires these of us in our obedience to Him. The first is to keep the mind in such a posture and framework that it is obedient and watchful against all sinful enticements. The second is to attend to and perform all particular actions as God requires according to His will. In these two things consist the whole duty of the mind of the believer. Indwelling sin tries to divert and to draw away the believer from doing these things.

This duty of the mind concerns two things. The first concerns God in His goodness and grace. The second concerns ourselves as sinners. Sin distracts us from both of these things and permits the law of sin to prosper within us to the best possible advantage.

Sin, then, endeavors to draw us away from a due consideration of God. As Jeremiah 2:19 declares: "Know therefore and see that it is an evil thing and bitter, that you have forsaken the LORD your God." Indeed, we forsake the Lord our God every time we sin. If the heart does not realize how wrong and how bitter are the results of forsaking God, then it will never remain secure against sin. God accepts the sinner who is in a humble, contrite, self-abasing disposition. "Thus says the high and lofty One, that inhabiteth eternity, whose name is Holy; I dwell in the high and holy place, with him also that is of a contrite and humble spirit, to revive the spirit of the humble, and to revive the heart of the contrite ones" (Isa. 57:15). This attitude is also seen in the Publican's prayer (Luke 18:13–14).

"Be clothed with humility" says the apostle (1 Peter 5:5). This is what becomes us as the only safe disposition. For he who walks humbly, walks safely. This is the purpose of Peter's advice, "Pass the time of your sojourning here in fear" (1 Peter 1:17). This is not a servile fear of bondage that upsets and perplexes the soul. It is the fear that keeps people calling constantly upon the Father in the light of final judgment. "If you call on the Father, who without respect of persons judgeth according to every man's work, pass the time of your sojourning here in fear." This is the humble frame of mind.

How is this humble disposition obtained? How is it kept? It is only achieved by a constant, deep apprehension of the evil, vileness, and danger of sin. The Publican prays, "God be merciful to me a sinner" (Luke 18:13). This sense of sin kept him humble. Humility led him to plead for pardon from sin.

In the case of Joseph we also see that to fear the effects of sin is to fear the Lord. "How then can I do this great wickedness, and sin against God?" (Gen. 39:9). Indeed, the fear of sin and the fear of the Lord are the same thing. "The fear of the Lord, that is wisdom; and to depart from evil is understanding" (Job 28:28).

If sin draws the soul away from the fear of the Lord, then it invades the soul secretly and makes it gradually insensitive to sin. There are two principal ways the law of sin endeavors to take the mind off this godly disposition.

1. Sin diverts the mind by emphasizing "cheap grace."

The gospel is never divorced from ethics. Not only is the gospel deliverance from the evil of sin, its filth, and its guilt, but it also leads us to discover what we ought to do. "The grace of God that bringeth salvation hath appeared to all men, teaching us that, denying ungodliness and worldly lusts, we should live soberly, righteously, and godly in this present world" (Titus 2:11–12). Holiness is thus called "a conversation that becomes the gospel" (Phil. 1:27). Its aim, end, and design are to make us live holy lives. When the word of the gospel is thus received, it produces holy living (see Rom. 12:2 and Eph. 4:20–24).

Here then is where the deceit of sin intervenes. It separates the doctrine of grace from its purpose. It persuades us to dwell upon the notion of grace and diverts our attention from the influence that grace gives to achieve its proper application in holy lives. From the doctrine of assured pardon of sin, it insinuates a carelessness for sin. God in Christ makes a true proposition, but Satan with sin makes a false conclusion.

To reprove this deceit, Paul says, "What shall we say then? Shall we continue in sin, that grace may abound? God forbid" (Rom. 6:1–2). "Man's deceitful heart," he is saying, "is apt to make that conclusion. But we should never entertain such a thought." On the other hand, Jude speaks of ungodly men, who turned "the grace of God into lasciviousness" (Jude 4).

The wisdom of faith and the power of grace oppose such deceit. The great effect of the gospel's wisdom and grace keeps the heart always in deep humility, in abhorrence to sin, and in self-abasement. This is the test of the real efficacy of the gospel: It keeps the heart humble, lowly, sensible to sin, and broken on that account. The Spirit of grace moves us to repentance and teaches us to detest sin. But if men remain secretly or insensibly loosened and relaxed in their thoughts of sin, then they cling to a false spirit of grace.

Sometimes we see men walking in a spirit of bondage, with little appreciation of the grace of God. It is difficult to determine whether they live under law or grace. On the one hand, they seem more sensitive to sinning than many who know more of the experience of grace. Yet the deceitfulness of sin diverts them from a consideration of the nature and danger of sin. This is done in several ways.

First, the soul—needing frequently to return to gospel grace because of guilt—allows grace to become commonplace and ordinary. Having found a good medicine for its wound, it then takes it for granted.

Second, the deceitfulness of sin takes advantage of the doctrine of grace to abuse it, stretching the soul's sense of liberty beyond the limit that God assigns. Some never feel free from legalism unless they indulge in sensuality and plunge into its depths. Sin pleads that certain limits are quite unnecessary. "Shouldn't the gospel relieve one of such narrow bounds?" they argue. But does this mean we should live as if the gospel was unnecessary or as though pardon of sin was nonessential?

Third, in times of temptation, the deceitfulness of sin goes to such lengths as to actually plead the need to sin, in order to show the reality of gospel grace. It pleads for this in two ways.

The first argument suggests that the new creature does not need to live so strictly. The manner of vigilance against sin is overly scrupulous, it argues.

The second argument contends that when sin is committed, it

is not so serious after all. It will not lead to the destruction of the soul, because it will be pardoned by the grace of the gospel. The truth is thus twisted into deception; and it is a source of temptation to sin once more. It becomes a deadly poison when it is thought to be a nourishing food. The mind thus becomes careless about sin, and the sense of sin's vileness is lost.

2. Sin deceives the mind from seeing the true state and condition of people in the world.

This is the second principal way sin diverts a godly frame of mind. People in their younger days naturally have more vigorous, active, and quick affections. As their minds begin to naturally slow down, the edge and keenness are lost. Nevertheless, unless they are steeped in sensuality or lustful corruptions, they will grow in their insights, resolutions, and judgments. If, however, their affections (or inclined and disciplined emotions) are not educated, they will become foolish old people. It is as if the weak tendencies of childhood are never corrected and lead to greater, more exaggerated forms of weakness in old age.

Thus the first priority of the Christian should begin with his affections. Just as these affections are great and large in natural youth, so they are spiritually great in spiritual youth. "I remember the kindness of thy youth, the love of thine espousals," says the prophet (Jer. 2:2). The deep wound of the conviction of sin and the healing of forgiveness stand out fresh and vivid in the memory and in the spirit of the newly converted. But later, with the decline of the affections, their spiritual sense also changes.

We see this in people who have never developed deep convictions in the ways of God. They become sensitive to sin for a time. They even weep and mourn in their guilt about sin. They make hearty and fervent resolutions against sin. But they are like grass that grows rapidly for a few days, but—with shallow rootage—quickly fades away. After a while, the more experience they have of sin, the less sensitive they become to its presence, as Ecclesiastes 8:11 describes. This happens because the awareness of sin in the emotions never becomes firmly fixed in their mind. Their mind remains preoccupied with the results of sin—sorrow, trouble, grief, fear—that give the mind no rest. But with no real conviction of sin itself, the soul lies in danger of hardening.

WEAKENING DECEIT BY MEDITATION AND PRAYER

It is the duty of the mind to keep the soul in a constant, holy concern for God and His grace. This is the essence of obedience to the gospel. Hence Scripture emphasizes the contrast between the mind filled with earthly things and the true need of being heavenly-minded. "Set your affection on things above, not on things on the earth" (Col. 3:2). It is as if the apostle says, "You cannot be occupied with both at the same time." The affections of the one proceed from principles that are opposed and inconsistent with the other.

We are also exhorted, "Love not the world, neither the things that are in the world. If any man love the world, the love of the Father is not in him" (1 John 2:15). "You cannot serve God and mammon" recognizes the contradiction between the lordship of one master over against the other (Matt. 6:24). Undue concern for earthly things is opposed to the true disposition toward godliness. On the other hand, all duties of obedience toward God flatly contradict sin.

But there are some godly duties that are particularly important in weakening and subduing the power of indwelling sin in the believers. These are first prayer and then meditation. They have much in common, differing only in the manner of their exercise. By meditation, I mean meditating upon what respect and relevance there is between the Word and our own heart, so that they stay close together in conformity to each other. As we ponder on the truth as it is in Jesus, we see how it is reflected in our own hearts. Thus meditation has the same intent as prayer, which is to bring our mind into a disposition that answers in all things to the mind and will of God.

Of the two, people are less familiar with—and therefore more confused about—meditation. So let us set two or three rules to help us in this matter.

1. Meditate about God with God.

When we think about God and His excellencies, glory, majesty, love, and goodness, let it be done in such a way that we are speaking directly to God, in a spirit of deep humility and dependence before Him. This will fix the mind and draw out one thing after the other that gives glory to God in a fitting manner. This will affect the soul to exercise a holy admiration of God and a delight in Him that is acceptable to God. Meditate as you would pray or give praise, speaking with God.

2. Meditate on the Word in the Word of God.

When reading the Scriptures, consider the particular sense of each passage. Look to God to find help, guidance, and direction in the discovery of His mind and will within the Scriptures. Then labor to have your heart affected by it.

3. Endeavor to meditate frequently.

When we come short of prolonged sustained concentration in meditation, let us make up by frequency in meditation. Some become discouraged because their minds do not provide them with a regular supply of thought to carry on their meditations. They are weak or imperfect in their reflections. Compensate for weakness here by frequently returning to the subject proposed for meditation. Thus new aspects will be discerned.

Although there are other spiritual duties, both meditation and prayer particularly oppose indwelling sin. They are always designing the destruction of sin. So we need to examine their importance further. First, we need to show the value of prayer and meditation. Later, we will see how the deceitfulness of sin distracts the mind from prayer and meditation.

We see the value of meditation and especially of prayer in several ways. First, this duty of the soul *reveals all the secret workings and actions of sin,* recognizing the danger it poses. David entitled one of his prayers, "A prayer of the afflicted, when he is overwhelmed, and poureth out his complaint before the LORD" (Ps. 102). This is a prayer concerning the soul's circumstances of need, frustration, and crisis. Without this, prayer is not prayer. For whatever show or appearance of duty we perform in prayer, without this realism of personal need prayer does not exist. Without this sense of need, our prayers are of no use to the glory of God or of any good to the souls of men. It is like a cloud without rain, driven by the wind of the mere breath of man. Nothing is more detrimental to the reality of true prayer than the mere thoughtless repetition of words.

The Spirit of God assists us to pray as we should. He reveals and shows to us the most secret actions and workings of the law of sin. "We know not what we should pray for as we ought: but the Spirit helps us in our infirmities" (Rom. 8:26). He discovers the basic need for which we need the most help and relief.

It is a fact of practical daily experience among believers that in prayer we discover and become convicted of the secret, deceitful work of sin in our hearts in a way we never could have otherwise. David, in Psalm 51, finds in prayer the wound of his soul searched by the Spirit of God and makes a discovery in verse 5 that he could never have made himself. "Behold, I was shapen in iniquity; and in sin did my mother conceive me." Like a candle in the darkness, the Holy Spirit illuminates the deep recesses of the heart, exposing the subtle and deceitful schemes and imaginations of sin. Thus the power of prayer penetrates sin and destroys it.

Therefore, it is the duty of the mind to "watch unto prayer" (1 Peter 4:7). We need to attend diligently to the state of our soul and to deal fervently and effectively with God about it. The same is true about meditation when we use it wisely for its real purpose.

Second, the effect of this *gives the heart a deep, full sense of the vileness of sin* and a constant renewed sense of detesting it. This is one purpose of prayer—to present sin before us, drawing out its vileness, abomination, and seriousness, so that it is loathed, abhorred, and therefore cast away as a filthy garment (see Isa. 30:22). He who pleads with God for the remission of sin also pleads with his own heart to detest it (see Hos. 14:2–3). In this way, sin is judged in the name of God. It also confirms to the soul that God detests sin and passes sentence. Prayer, then, sensitizes our soul against sin, so that it will not be bribed or confirmed secretly by sin for even a moment. This leads to the weakening of indwelling sin in the believer.

Third, prayer is the way appointed and blessed by God to *obtain strength and power against sin.* Does any man lack? "Let him ask of God" (James 1:5). Through prayer we obtain a supply for all our wants and the assistance against all opposition, especially that which is made against us by sin. There is where we find "help in time of need" (Heb. 4:16).

Fourth, prayer and meditation *counteract all the deceitful workings of sin* and, therefore, remain constantly engaged with God in conflict to all sin. "I have sworn," says the psalmist, "and I will perform it, that I will keep Thy righteous judgments"

(Ps. 119:106). This is the language of every gracious soul in its address to God, from the intimacy of cleaving to Him in all things to opposing sin in all things. He who cannot do, cannot pray. To pray with any other frame of mind is to flatter God with our lips, which God abhors.

We have seen four ways in which the spirit of true prayer helps the believer to destroy sin. First, it exposes any secret sin lurking in the heart. Like wild beasts, the more earnestly they are pursued, the more likely will they be discovered. Second, prayer weakens a prevalent sin and develops an antidote to it. When the soul of the believer becomes sick with spontaneous languor or apparently causeless weariness, it is a sure sign some sinful disease remains within the soul. Third, as long as the soul engages itself with God, it is certain sin cannot rise up in ruinous dominance. "I was also upright before him, and he kept me from iniquity" (Ps. 18:23). Finally, when the heart remains undeceived by sin in its diligence before God, it receives a special diligence and watchfulness against sin.

DISTRACTIONS FROM MEDITATION, PRAYER, AND OTHER DUTIES

Sin seeks to divert the mind from God in various ways. This principally happens when sin argues that certain things are necessary and lawful for the mind to dwell on. All who excused themselves from the marriage feast did so because of lawful pursuits—one for his farm, another for his oxen (see Luke 14:16–19). By this excuse, their minds were drawn away from that disposition of heavenly-mindedness that is required in our walk with God. What wisdom and vigilance we need to avoid such seducing reasoning. This, then, is the first and most general attempt indwelling sin makes upon the soul in deception. It draws away the mind from a diligent attention to the seriousness of sin; it keeps the mind from maintaining a due and constant regard for God and His grace.

The division sin makes in the mind also affects our significant duties. Sin, indeed, maintains an enmity against all duties of obedience and indeed against God Himself. "When I would do good," admits the apostle, "evil is present with me" (Rom. 7:21). That is to say, "Whenever I would do what is spiritually good for God's honor and glory, sin is present in me to hinder me from doing it." There are four ways, then, that sin seeks to accomplish its ends.

1. Sin takes advantage of the weariness of the flesh.

Since the law of sin is adverse to all communion with God, no relief aids the soul as long as sin indwells the believer. The soul becomes like one traveling alone without companions or diversions, making the journey seem long. The Savior declares to the sleeping disciples in the Garden, "The spirit indeed is willing, but the flesh is weak" (Matt. 26:41). Out of that weakness grew their weariness to pray. God complains of His people, "You have been weary with me" (Isa. 43:22). This weariness may reach the climax described in Malachi 1:13—"You have said, Behold, what a weariness is this! You have sniffed at it, says the LORD of hosts."

The deceit lies in the compliance between the spiritual flesh and the natural flesh. Together they are averse to God and generate weakness. The spouse in Song of Solomon 5:2–3 sleeps spiritually. She also expresses her reluctance to rise from her resting place.

2. The deceitfulness of sin argues falsely about the pressing circumstances in life.

Should we always pray and meditate, even when we neglect our other duties and thus become useless to ourselves and to others in the world? On this reasoning, particular duties readily dispose of the general practice of prayer. Men lack the leisure to glorify God and save their own souls.

Yet no duties need constantly to jostle other duties aside. Special occasions must be determined by special circumstances. But if we take more time than necessary to perform some duty, we rob God of the time He deserves and we need for our own souls. God will not bless us in that activity. It is important that all other duties remain subservient to our regard of God and His holiness. Yet so readily does the deceitfulness of sin use duties to rob God of His due.

3. Sin argues for compensatory duties.

Sin draws away the attention of the mind by focusing on the need to do some specific duty. In this way Saul forgot his disobedience to God by making sacrifice (see 1 Sam. 13:9). The repression of this essential duty by the substitution of another ensnares the heart. The corrupt reasonings of sin should motivate us to watch and pray.

4. Sin feeds the soul with false promises and purposes.

Felix used this device when he said to Paul, "Go thy way for this time; when I have a more convenient season, I will call for thee" (Acts 24:25). In this way, the present time, which is all we possess as our own, becomes irrevocably lost.

These are some of the ways the mind diverts from its duty, leading to the further entanglement of the affections and the understanding. When sin operates in this manner, a man is "drawn away" or diverted from what he should attend to constantly in his walk before the Lord.

Consider the beginning of your failings in the ways of God. Like an illness, when we see how it starts, we are able to seek a cure more intelligently. The principal care and charge of the soul, as we have seen, lie then in the mind. If the mind fails in its duty, it is like a sentry who fails in his duty. All is lost because of his negligence.

If you want to test yourself but have failed to determine how sin deceives you, look to see what you have fallen into. In one way or another, you have become heedless, indifferent, lazy, uncertain, and deceived from doing your duty. Consider then the charge of Proverbs 4:23–27.

May your soul never respond and say, "If I had attend more diligently and considered more wisely the vile nature of sin, and if I had not allowed my mind to be possessed by such vain hopes and delusions or allowed my mind to be filled with the things of the world to the neglect of my spiritual duties, then I would not now be so vile, weak, thriftless, wounded, decadent, and defiled. It was my careless and deceived mind that brought about the sin and transgression of my soul." Yet let such reflection lead to healing and restoration, which the performance of duties alone will never bring about (see Ps. 23:3).

The right disposition of mind keeps us generally in the mind and will of God. It is a vital grace to have "the spirit of power, and of love, and of a sound mind" (2 Tim. 1:7). The stable, solid, resolved mind in the things of God is not easily moved, diverted, changed, or drawn aside. It is a mind that is not prone to listen to corrupt reasonings, false insinuations, or pretexts seeking to draw it away from its duty.

The apostle exhorts us to be "stedfast, unmoveable, always abounding in the work of the Lord"(1 Cor. 15:58). The steadfast mind keeps on duty, producing stability and fruitfulness by its obedience. On the other hand, Peter tells us that those who are deceived and enticed fall from their own steadfastness (2 Peter 3:17). The great weakness of the backslider is his lack of stead-fastness. "Their heart was not ... stedfast" (Ps. 78:37). The true nature of such steadfastness is first, a full purpose of cleaving to God; second, a daily renewal and quickening of heart to discharge each duty; and third, a resolution not to neglect such duties.

HOW THE MIND IS DIVERTED FROM SPECIFIC DUTIES

We have not yet come to grips with the way sin actually diverts the mind from its duty. This is vital to consider because of its importance in affecting the soul and the conscience. First, if the mind is drawn away, tainted, weakened, and negligent of its role, then the whole soul is affected. For this reason the apostle exhorts us, "We ought to give the more earnest heed to the things which we have heard, lest at any time we should let them slip" (Heb. 2:1). When sin affects our mind by deceitfulness we lose the life, power, sense, and impression of the Word. This is most serious; it is cause for the greatest concern in our souls.

In addition, because the mind works spiritually[1] in the soul it needs to be stirred and enlightened. The conscience is not apt to be aroused if the mind fails to warn the soul. When sin entangles the emotions or the will chooses to sin, the conscience becomes violently aroused if the mind remains keen. But the mind can be subtly and gradually neglected spiritually; without special attention, it goes unnoticed. Sin uses at least six ways to so distract the mind.

1. Sin persuades the mind to deal in generalities and to avoid particular duties.

Sin sometimes even persuades the soul to glorify God in a general way. Thus Saul in a vague sense did the will of God in fighting the war with Amalek, yet at the same time, he dishonored God (see 1 Sam. 15). It is pointless for a man to assume he is traveling in the right direction when he ignores all the signs along the way. It is in particular actions where we express and exercise our faith and obedience.

2. The mind feels content in performance of its duties while secretly sinning.

After his military expeditions against Amalek, Saul says to Samuel, "I have performed the commandment of the LORD" (1 Sam. 15:13). The Israelites ask, "Wherefore have we fasted, and thou seest not?" (Isa. 58:3). Because they felt pleased in their performance before the Lord, they also assumed God was pleased! But they failed God miserably. The deceitfulness of sin diverts us from glorifying God to finding satisfaction with our own pursuits.

3. The mind often becomes perfunctory in its perform-ance of duties.

But such a manner, says Amos, is not a disposition toward God (Amos 5:21–25). None of the people offered sacrifices for *God*, although they made this claim. This, then, is why professors do not thrive in the performance of all their duties. They experience little or no real communion with God because they become distracted by business and remain blind to the real purpose of their actions. In this way, many duties of worship and obedience—performed by a woeful generation of hypocrites, formalists, and secular persons—lack both life and light. These duties are not acceptable to God because the worshipers live estranged from God.

4. Sin distracts the mind from maintaining its diligence.

When sin succeeds, it produces spiritual sloth. The biblical commands to *watch* warn against this danger. "I say unto you all, Watch" (Mark 13:37). Use your utmost diligence not to be surprised and deceived. "Consider your ways" (Hag. 1:5, 7). God complains that the Israelites failed to do this (Deut. 32:29). Hebrews 6:11–12 declares, "We desire that every one of you do show the same diligence to the full assurance of hope unto the end: That ye be not slothful." Likewise, Peter exhorts, "And beside this, giving all diligence, add to your faith virtue; and to virtue knowledge ..." (2 Peter 1:5). Scripture exhorts us to use our utmost diligence to escape sin's deceit.

When a man fails to watch for sin's deceit, he becomes spiritually lazy. Scripture points out four characteristics of spiritual sloth. First, there is *inadvertency*. As the writer to the Hebrews says, such a person is "dull of hearing" (Heb. 5:11). A secret carelessness has crept into his spirit.

Second, there is an *unwillingness to be stirred up to do his duty*. "A slothful man hideth his hand in his bosom, and will not so much as bring it to his mouth again" (Prov. 19:24). When special calls and warnings are given, he does not respond to perform his duties.

Third, there are the *weak and ineffectual attempts to recover himself and to complete his tasks*. "As the door turns upon its hinges, so the slothful man turns upon his bed" (Prov. 26:14). He feebly starts many tasks, but he never finishes them.

Finally, there is the *lack of moral fortitude to overcome difficulties and discouragement*. "The slothful man says, There is a lion without, I shall be slain in the streets" (Prov. 22:13). Every difficulty deters him from his duty. He thinks it is impossible to even try.

5. Sin distracts the mind by using deceit to take it by surprise.

Thus, when sin caught Peter off guard by the dangers he feared, he forgot the love and warning of Christ. Likewise, when sin caught up David by lusts and temptations, he forgot the principles by which he formerly lived. We should exercise wisdom not to parley with sin. It will only surprise the soul with an unexpected attack.

6. Sin deceives the mind by frequent and lengthy solicitations.

It persists until it finally makes a conquest. We therefore must never cease our vigilance. We need a watchful disposition of spirit all the time. We must keep all of these things in mind, lest sin divert and deceive us.

HOW THE MIND IS DIRECTED TO SPECFIC DUTIES

For the right performance of our duty, it is not enough to "perform." When we build a house, we busy ourselves with gathering all the stone and timber together in one great heap. But we must understand and appreciate the architect's drawings to properly construct the building. In the same way we often busy ourselves with various rules and regulations. But if we do not have the appropriate spirit to perform these duties, our effort is in vain. "To what purpose is the multitude of your sacrifices?" (Isa. 1:11). "They are a trouble to me; I am weary to bear them" (1:14).

We need to live according to an overall design or rule. Paul mentions this in Galatians 6:16 ("as many as walk according to this rule"). It is only appropriate to link duty with a proper attitude. When Paul says, "walk circumspectly" (Eph. 5:15), he refers to this attitude and disposition of heart and mind. Four things may be said about this rule or attitude.

1. We must obey God wholeheartedly.

The law did not permit a beast to be sacrificed if it had a defect. The animal had to be whole. The priests rejected any animal that was deficient, blind, or lame. It is the same with God's duties. They must be sound and whole. If we seek to obey God with mixed motives, our duties will not be acceptable.

2. We must depend on God in faith to obey Him.

We must perform our duties in faith, deriving our strength from Christ, without whom we "can do nothing" (John 15:5). It is not enough to believe, though that is necessary in every good work (see Eph. 2:10). Faith must characterize our obedience. Paul describes this as "the obedience of faith" (Rom. 1:5). Only then will we see how Christ is "our life" (Col. 3:4)—the spring, source, and cause of our spiritual life. We experience and know this in faith. Thus Paul says, "Christ liveth in me: and the life which I now live in the flesh I live by the faith of the Son of God" (Gal. 2:20). Christ is our life, and He is also the source of our obedience in the discharge of all our duties of holiness.

3. We must exercise our understanding and affections to obey God.

First, God prescribes the manner and means in which we are to obey Him. Unless this is recognized, the whole performance of our duty is invalidated. This is why God often exhorts us to do things *wisely* as well as diligently. Second, the affections of the heart and mind profoundly influence the way we perform our duties. Indeed, every duty must be performed with spiritual affections. Otherwise, it is like a sacrifice without the heart, without salt, without fire. It is useless. He who gives with cheerfulness recognizes this disposition (see 2 Cor. 9:7).

4. We must obey God to bring Him glory.

What other good reasons do we consider for performing our duties? Perhaps we think of the satisfaction of our own convictions and consciences. Or perhaps we think of the praise of men to arouse our self-righteousness and its excessive displays. These reasons only sidetrack us. Instead, the apostle says, "Do all to the glory of God" (1 Cor. 10:31). Much of sin's deceit lies in distracting us from this primary objective.

Right attitudes enable us to perform our duties properly. Similarly, right thoughts protect us from the diversions of sin. Five considerations may be noted to direct our mind against the deceit that hinders us from fulfilling our duties.

1. We must consider the sovereignty of God.

This is the first reason we should develop a sensitivity to sin. Joseph asks, "How can I do this great wickedness, and sin against God?" (Gen. 39:9). Potiphar's wife tempted Joseph to ignore the graciousness of his master (see 39:7–9). But much more important, Joseph knew fornication was sin against God. Likewise, James tells us that in our dealing with anything contrary to the law, it is the Lawgiver Himself who should be our first concern (see James 4:11–12). In all lusts and temptations, then, our first thought should recall, "It is God Himself who forbids this thing. He is the One under whose absolute sovereignty I live and on whom my present and eternal conditions depend."

2. We must consider the punishment of sin.

Job acknowledges, "Destruction from God was a terror to me, and by reason of his highness I could not endure" (Job 31:23). Likewise, the apostle reminds us, "It is a fearful thing to fall into the hands of the living God" (Heb. 10:31). He also said, "Vengeance is mine, I will repay" (10:30). He is a sin-avenging God who "will by no means clear the guilty" (Exod. 34:7). "Our God is a consuming fire" (Heb. 12:29), so we shall consider His holiness and justice. What life is there for those who know it is "the judgment of God, that they which commit such things are worthy of death," yet they continue in them? (Rom. 1:32).

3. We must consider the love and kindness of God against whom sin is committed.

This is a prevailing consideration if it is rightly and graciously objective in the soul. Moses challenged the people: "Do ye thus requite the LORD, O foolish people and unwise? is not he thy father that hath bought thee? hath he not made thee, and established thee?" (Deut. 32:6).

With the same consideration, the apostle argues, "Having therefore these promises, dearly beloved, let us cleanse ourselves from all filthiness of the flesh and spirit, perfecting holiness in the fear of God" (2 Cor. 7:1). Here Paul refers to the promise that God will be a Father unto us and receive us (see 2 Cor. 6:17–18). This promise speaks of all God's love, both now and through eternity. Surely this is a strong motivation not to sin, is it not? In 1 John 3:1–3 the love of the Father motivates us as well. The apostle says, "Everyone who has this hope purifies himself" (3:3). He abstains from all sin.

Likewise, special and particular mercies of His love should keep us mindful of who God is in the hour of temptation. Solomon sinned greatly by ignoring the special mercies of God. He sinned after God had "appeared twice to him" (1 Kings 11:9).

4. We must consider the blood and mediation of Christ.

The apostle declares, "The love of Christ constraineth us; because we thus judge, that if one died for all, then were all dead: and that he died for all, that they which live should not henceforth live unto themselves, but unto him which died for them, and rose again" (2 Cor. 5:14–15). There is a constraining efficacy in this consideration. It is great, forcible, and effective when it is heeded.

5. We must consider the indwelling Holy Spirit.

This surely is the greatest privilege we have in this world. We need to consider how He is grieved by sin and how we defile His dwelling place. We must guard against forfeiting or even despising His comforts. Careful meditation upon these considerations helps to keep us from sin and temptation.

NOTES

[1] Our mind is often spoken of in Scripture as our "spirit." We find this in Romans 1:9 ("whom I serve with my spirit") and in 1 Thessalonians 5:23 ("your whole spirit and soul"—that is to say, your mind and affections). It is true that in the context of gifts, *spirit* is used in distinction to the mind (1 Cor. 14:15). But when *spirit* is applied to the faculty of the soul, it means the mind.

CHAPTER 4

THE ENTICEMENT OF INDWELLING SIN

Sin not only deceives; it also entices. People are drawn away "and enticed" (James 1:14). Sin draws the *mind* away from a duty, but it entices the *emotions*. We will consider three things: sin's enticement of the emotions, how sin accomplishes this, and our need to guard our affections because of this danger.

The affections are snared when they are aroused by sin. For when sin prevails, it captures the affections completely within it. Sin continually obsesses the imaginations with possessive images. The wicked "devise iniquity, and work evil upon their beds," which they also practice when they are given the chance (Mic. 2:1). Peter says they have "eyes full of adultery, and they cannot cease from sin" (2 Peter 2:14). Their imagination continually fills their soul with the objects of their lusts.

The apostle describes the things in the world as "the lust of the flesh, the lust of the eyes, and the pride of life" (1 John 2:16). The lust of the eyes enters the soul, forcing the imagination to portray its intentions. John speaks of this as the lust of the "eyes" because it constantly represents these images to the mind and to the soul, just as our natural eyes present images of outward objects to the brain.

Indeed, the actual sight of the eyes often occasions these imaginations. Achan declared how sin had prevailed over him in Joshua 7:21. First, he *saw* the gold and the Babylonian garments;

then he *coveted* them. Seeing them, he imagined their value to him, and then he fixed them in his desiring heart.

The enticement of sin is heightened when the imagination dominates over the mind. It implants vain thoughts within the mind and delights secretly in its complacency. When we indulge with delight in thoughts of forbidden things, we commit sin, even though our will has not yet consented to perform the deed. The prophet asks, "How long will your vain thoughts lodge within you?" (Jer. 4:14). All these thoughts come and go as messengers, carrying sin with them. Such thoughts inflame the imagination and entangle the affections more and more.

As we have already seen, sin always seeks to extenuate and lessen the seriousness of sin to the mind. "It is only a small offense," it says. "It will be given up shortly." With such excuses it speaks the language of a deceived heart. When there is a readiness on the part of the soul to listen to these silent voices—secret insinuations that arise from deceit—it is evident that the affections are already enticed.

When the soul willingly listens to these seductions, it has already lost its affections for Christ and has become seduced. Sin entices like "wine when it is red, when it gives its colour in the cup, when it moves itself attractively" (Prov. 23:31). But in the end, sin "bites like a serpent, and stings like an adder" (23:32).

How, then, does sin deceive to entice and to entangle the affections? First, it *makes use of the tendency of the mind.* If the mind is like a sly bird, sin will not capture it. "Surely in vain the net is spread in the sight of any bird" (Prov. 1:17). But if a bird is distracted, its wings are of little use to escape from the trap. Thus does sin entice. It diverts the mind away from the danger by false reasonings and pretenses, then casts its net upon the affections to entangle them.

Second, sin takes advantage of the phases of life and *proposes sin to be desirable.* It gilds over an object with a thousand pretenses that the imagination promotes as "the *pleasures* of sin" (Heb. 11:25). Unless one despises these pleasures, as Moses did, one cannot escape from them. Those who live in sin, the apostle says, "live in pleasure" (James 5:5). It is pleasure because it suits the flesh to lust after them. Hence the caution given, "Make no provision for the flesh, to fulfil the lusts thereof" (Rom. 13:14). That is to say, do not nourish yourself with the lusts of the flesh, which sin gives to you through your thoughts or affections. He also warns us, "Fulfil not the lusts of the flesh" (Gal. 5:16). When men live under the power of sin, they fulfill "the desires of the flesh and of the mind" (Eph. 2:3). When sin would entangle the soul, it prevails with the imagination to solicit the heart by painting sin as something beautiful and satisfying.

Third, it *hides the danger* associated with sin. Sin covers the hook with bait, and spreads the food over the net. It is, of course, impossible for sin to completely remove the knowledge of danger from the soul. It cannot remove the reality that "the wages of sin is death" (Rom. 6:23) or hide "the judgment of God, that they who commit sin are worthy of death" (Rom. 1:32). But it so takes up and possesses the mind and affections with the attraction and desirability of sin, that it diverts the soul from realizing its danger.

In the account of the fall of man, Eve properly told the serpent, "If we eat or touch the fruit of that tree, we shall die" (Gen. 3:3). But Satan immediately filled her mind with the beauty and usefulness of the fruit, and she quickly forgot her practical concern for the consequences of eating. Likewise, David became so caught up in his lusts that he ignored the consequences of his great sin. It is said he "despised the LORD" (2 Sam. 12:9).

When sin tempts with such pressure, it uses a thousand wiles to hide the soul from the terror of the Lord. Hopes of pardon will be used to hide it. Future repentance also covers it, as well as the present insistence of lust and the particular occasion or opportunity. Sin uses many other excuses: extenuating circumstances, surprise, the balance of duties, the obsession of the imagination, and desperate resolutions. It uses a thousand such excuses.

Sin then proceeds to present arguments to the mind in order to conceive the desired sin. This we will consider in the next chapter.

Let us look now at the remedies for avoiding such deception of sin. Clearly, we need to watch our affections. The Scriptures say: "Keep your heart with all diligence" (Prov. 4:23). We keep our heart in two ways.

First, we guard our affections by mortifying our members (see Col. 3:5). The apostle is saying, "You are to prevent the working and deceit of sin, which is in your members." He also says, "Set your affection on things above, not on things on the earth" (3:2). Fixing and filling your affections with heavenly things will mortify sin.

What are the objects of such affections? They include God Himself, in His beauty and glory; the Lord Jesus Christ, who is "altogether lovely ... the chiefest of ten thousand" (Song. 5:10, 16); grace and glory; the mysteries of the gospel; and the blessings promised by the gospel. If these were the preoccupation of our affections, what scope would sin have to tempt and enter into our hearts? (See 2 Cor. 4:17–18.)

Second, let us fix our affections on the cross of Christ. Paul says, "God forbid that I should glory, save in the cross of our Lord Jesus Christ, whereby the world is crucified unto me, and I unto the world" (Gal. 6:14). When someone sets his affections upon the cross and the love of Christ, he crucifies the world as a dead and undesirable thing. The baits of sin lose their attraction and disappear. Fill your affections with the cross of Christ, and you will find no room for sin. The world put Him out of a house and into a stable, when He came to save us. Let Him now turn the world out-of-doors, when He comes to sanctify us.

Remember also that the vigor of our affections toward heavenly things is apt to decline unless it is constantly looked after, exercised, directed, and warned. God speaks often in Scripture of those who lost their first love, allowing their affections to decay. Let us be jealous over our hearts to prevent such backsliding.

CHAPTER 5

THE CONCEPTION OF INDWELLING SIN

Sin not only deceives and entices. It also conceives. James says, "When lust hath conceived, it bringeth forth sin" (James 1:15). It comes to fruition. In terms of the psychology of the soul, this means that the consent of the will has now been gained. When this takes place, it is like a woman who loses her virginity, instead of remaining chaste toward God in Christ (see 2 Cor. 11:2–3). Four aspects of this conception merit our consideration.

1. The will is the cause of obedience or disobedience.

Moral actions are willed. An ancient sage said: "Every sin is so voluntary, that if it is not voluntary, it is not sin." The will actualizes sin or obedience.

2. The will consents to sin.

The will does this in two ways. Sometimes, after full and complete deliberation, the will becomes wholly convinced, weakened, or conquered. With this general, overall consent, the will goes to sea like a ship in full sail. Or it rushes into sin like a horse into battle. People do this, says the apostle, "giving themselves over to sin with greediness" (Eph. 4:19). Ahab, for example, deliberately murdered Naboth (see 1 Kings 21).

On the other hand, someone's will to sin may come in conflict with his other desires. Peter's will to deny his Master conflicted with his love for Christ. If he had not willed to deny Him, he would not have done so. Even then, he did not deny Christ with pleasure, but rather with grief and repentance (see Matt. 26:75).

3. The will may not completely consent to sin.

No Christian will absolutely and fully consent to sin, because within his will resides the principle to do good. The apostle spoke of this, saying, "I would do good" (Rom. 7:21). The principle of grace within a Christian inclines him toward good. Grace rules, not sin, in the believer. Though his will may consent to sin, it only does so partially, never absolutely.

The will does have a secret reluctance to commit sin. True, the soul does not always remain sensitive to this reluctance, and so sin carries it away temporarily. But the general principle holds that "the Spirit lusteth against the flesh" (Gal. 5:17). It does not always achieve the same degree of success. But this hesitation of the will to fall into sin often keeps the soul from sinning. Much wisdom lies then in the right discernment of the reluctance of the will to commit sin.

4. The will may be conditioned by tendencies.

Repeated acts of the will to sin often produce a disposition and inclination toward sin. This proneness leads to easy consent. We must exercise great care to watch against such a condition in our soul.

HOW THE WILL CONSENTS TO SIN

Where there is no will, as we have seen, there is no sin. How then does the deceit of sin lead to the consent of the will? To answer this, let us consider three truths.

1. The will consents to sin as a result of sin's deception.

The conception of sin always occurs as the result of some deception. Sin seeks to mix up the emotions, or mislead the reasoning,
or weaken the will in some way.

Sin manipulates the will with deception in a number of ways
and circumstances. Sin commonly "evaluates" grace into a pardon, making one assume mercy is always available for further
sinning. This abuse of grace deceives the mind and opens the
will's consent, removing the sense of evilness from evil. In
worldly hands, this deception prevails so much that they think
their liberty consists of acting as "servants of corruption" (2 Peter
2:19). Scripture warns that this poison also taints and corrupts
the minds of believers.

Grace contains a twofold mystery: We are not only to walk
with God, but also to go *to* God. The great aim of sin is to change
these purposes of grace and thus hinder the influence of grace.
The apostle therefore says, "These things write I unto you, that
ye sin not. And if any man sin, we have an advocate with the
Father, Jesus Christ the righteous: And he is the propitiation for
our sins" (1 John 2:1–2). The purpose of the gospel in its essence
is "that ye sin not." We are to walk with God.

But as long as we are in the world, we know this will not
always happen. John says, "If we say we have no sin, we deceive
ourselves, and the truth is not in us" (1:8). Yet he also adds, "If
any man sin, we have an advocate with the Father, Jesus Christ
the righteous: And he is the propitiation for our sins." Here is the
remedy when we fail to walk with God. We have access to God
for pardon and for further encouragement.

But sin deceives the mind and diverts it from these two true
purposes of the gospel and imposes upon the will to win its consent. It does this in various ways. One way is to come in sudden
temptation. Sin presents temptation as an immediate good, a

particular good, or a tangible good. Normally grace should rise up in the soul to reject the temptation. But if sin suddenly deceives the mind, sweeping it off its guard, then the will falls as well, even though a deed may never be committed. In the sight of God, however, sin is conceived at that moment.

Temptation sometimes arises gradually. Little by little it insinuates the poison until it gradually prevails. Cast into a false frame of reasoning, the soul turns against the grace of the gospel, and the will becomes spiritually debauched.

Sin also seeks to alleviate its own sense of guilt. It may seek to do so absolutely, arguing that the evil tendency is not so bad after all. Or sin may absolve itself by comparing itself with others. This is another major sphere of deception. By these and other means, sin seeks to evade recognition of its true character.

2. The will chooses the good and consents to nothing unless it has the appearance of good.

This may be an immediate good, or a temporary good, or the appearance of goodness, or the circumstances of what is good. Yet good is the will's natural and necessary object.

But when sin deceives the mind, it paints what is absolutely evil as having an apparently good appearance. This happened to Eve when she cast aside all considerations of the law, the covenant, and the warnings of God, to reflect on the advantages, pleasures, and benefits that she reckoned could be obtained by sin. Likewise, Ahab argued, "Naboth's vineyard is near my house, and I need it to make a garden of herbs; therefore I must have it" (1 Kings 21:2). Sin uses these arguments in a deceived mind to impose on one's will, until a person does not even stop short of murder—to the utter ruin of himself and his family.

3. The will operates as a rational appetite.

Rationally, it is guided by the mind. As an appetite, it is also excited by the emotions. It is influenced in its exercise by both of these faculties.

As we have seen in James 1:14–15, the conception of sin occurs by the consent of the will after sin entices the affections and deceives the mind.

In chapter 4 we considered how sin entices the affections to gain the consent of the will. Sometimes it does so hastily and impulsively by violent provocation. David acted with such impetuousness over the affair with Nabal. At first he was angry (see 1 Sam. 25:13). Then he became determined to destroy the whole family (see 25:33–34). He conceived murder in his heart, and it was only by God's mercy that he was kept from carrying out his intent. Peter also acted impulsively on more than one occasion. Sin conceives suddenly when it obtains the quick consent of the will.

On the other hand, sin may entice the affections to procure the consent of the will by frequent urgings, until gradually they dominate. Jacob's sons hated Joseph because their father loved him. This lay rankling in their hearts until they determined to kill him. Hatred and envy obsessed them until their will consented to his ruin. Once the will is ready to consent, then sin is conceived.

Sin also takes advantage of the darkness of the mind to work out its design and intentions. We discussed this in chapter 3. A darkened mind is totally devoid of saving grace. It only produces the "works of darkness" (Rom. 13:12; Eph. 5:11). Christians also have some darkness abiding within them, for they "know but in part" (1 Cor. 13:12). This darkness produces either ignorance (a beginner's knowledge of the will of God) or error.

If someone remains ignorant of the will of God, sin exploits that ignorance. Abimelech, for example, although a man of integrity, knew nothing of fornication as a sin (see Gen. 20:5). God states that His people "are destroyed for lack of knowledge" (Hos. 4:6). Many—ignorant of the instruction that they would give their family—complain about the public education system, when their own ignorance and moral indifference are to blame. Sin uses such ignorance to its best advantage.

Error is an even worse aspect of the mind's darkness. It gives great advantage to sin. When people become zealous for some error, they will suppress the truth and persecute it. Indwelling sin can have no greater help than this. The gentle Holy Spirit withdraws from such people and leaves them to the darkness of their errors.

SOME WAYS GOD PREVENTS THE FRUITION OF SIN

The text under consideration is James 1:15—"when lust hath conceived, it bringeth forth sin." Some interpret this to mean that as soon as sin is conceived, it comes to fruition.

Yet our argument has been that the conception of sin depends on the consent of the will, not on the actual commission of sin. Conception and commission do not automatically follow. There is a world of sin conceived in the womb of the wills and hearts of men that is never brought forth. Our inquiry now is to see how it is actualized.

That sin is not actualized is no merit to sin itself. What sin conceives it wills to bring forth. When someone willfully determines to perform some sinful deed, he has already committed sin by that very determination. Certain obstacles, however, mercifully prevent sin from always coming to fruition autonomously.

Sin comes to fruition whenever both the power and the will to sin continue together. What hinders sin from coming forth must affect either the power or the will of the sinner. God works to affect both. By His providence He obstructs the power of sin. By His grace He diverts or changes the will to sin. God's providence appears in His outward actions, and His grace works inwardly to change lives.

1. God's providence in outward acts obstructs the power of sin.

Life is the foundation of all power. As the vital principle, when life ceases, all power ceases, too. So God is known as "the living God" whose power never ceases (Deut. 5:26; Rev. 7:2). God frequently cuts short the power of sin by taking away the lives of those who persist in sin.

God promised, despite the threat of Sennacherib's army, "the Lord shall not deliver Jerusalem into his hand" (2 Kings 18:35). God threatened to cut short Sennacherib's power (see 19:28), which He did by taking away the lives of his soldiers (see 19:35). Without the soldiers, Sennacherib became powerless to bring forth the sin he conceived.

Pharaoh is another example of this principle. Moses complains: "The enemy said, I will pursue, I will overtake, I will divide the spoil; my lust shall be satisfied upon them; I will draw my sword, my hand shall destroy them" (Exod. 15:9). Then Moses sings: "You have blown with your wind, the sea covered them: they sank as lead in the mighty waters" (15:10). Similarly, God dealt with the companies of fifties and their captains that came to arrest Elijah (see 2 Kings 1:9–12). Fire came down from heaven and destroyed them.

Men in the earlier narratives of Genesis had hundreds of years to conceive and to bring forth sin, filling the world with violence, injustice, and chaos (see Gen. 6:5–13). God decreed,

"Blood-thirsty and deceitful men shall not live out half their days" (Ps. 55:23). God shortened the course of the pilgrimage of men on this earth in order to prevent an inundation of evil.

"Though a sinner do evil a hundred times, and his days be prolonged, yet surely I know that it shall be well with them that fear God, which fear before him. But it shall not be well with the wicked, neither shall he prolong his days, which are as a shadow; because he feareth not before God" (Eccl. 8:12–13). However long a wicked man may live, he will die *judiciously.*

Christians may believe God only cuts short the lives of unbelieving sinners. To them God is patient, as 2 Peter 3:9 declares. In His patience, He seeks their acknowledgment and repentance of every known sin. But in their thinking, God only cuts off those who never repent and who thus perish forever. When David repented, he prayed, "O spare me, that I may recover strength, before I go hence, and be no more" (Ps. 39:13).

Yet sometimes God does take away the lives of His own people to prevent them from incurring further guilt. First, in the coming of some great temptation and trial upon the world, God knows that certain believers could not hold out against it and thus would dishonor Him and defile themselves. Isaiah 57:1 declares, "The righteous is taken away from the evil to come." Second, God takes away those who persist in ignorance of God's mind and will. This seems to have been the case of Josiah (see 2 Chron. 35).

God also reduces or eradicates the power of sinners in other ways than in the elimination of life. In the case of the builders of Babel, God destroyed their power by confusing their language (see Gen. 11:6–9). In the case of the Sodomites, God smote them with blindness because of the filth of their lusts (see Gen. 19:11). When Jeroboam stretched out his hand to seize the prophet, God paralyzed it (see 1 Kings 13:4). Many a wretch in his or her lust has become diseased through such lusting.

In Psalm 64:6 the psalmist says, "They search out iniquities; they accomplish a diligent search: both the inward thought of every one of them, and the heart, is deep." They are ready and well prepared for much sinning. "But God shall shoot at them with an arrow; suddenly they shall be wounded. So they shall make their own tongue to fall upon themselves" (64:7–8).

Men go on sinning until they become "like a troubled sea that cannot rest" (Isa. 57:20). Jehoshaphat schemed against the will of God to make an alliance with Ahaziah and send ships with him to Tarshish. But God destroyed the ships in a storm so that he could not accomplish his design (see 2 Chron. 20:35–37).

God seems to intervene in this way only in cases of extraordinary temptation. He stops His people when Satan catches them in his violence and craft. Yet God ordinarily deals in this manner with the wicked. He catches them like "a wild bull in a net" (Isa. 51:20). God also deals with His people through disappointments, to make them reflect on their condition and actions.

God sometimes lets a sinner go on sinning, but raises up a contrary power to deal with him. When Saul determined to slay Jonathan, the people were aroused by God to oppose the fury of Saul and so deliver Jonathan (see 1 Sam. 14:45). Likewise, when King Uzziah presumptuously determined to offer incense (despite the teachings of the law), he was restrained by eighty priests, who drove him out of the temple (see 2 Chron. 26:16–20). In Revelation 12 the dragon and his allies seek furiously to destroy the church. But God stirs up the earth to come to her assistance. In Hosea 2:6–7 the people in their disloyalty to God sought their lovers. God left them alone to pursue this folly, yet He set up limitations so that they could not fulfill their lusts.

God also blocks the accomplishment of planned sin by

removing the desired object. God delivered Peter from Herod's spiteful plan to kill him by enabling him to escape from prison (see Acts 12:1–11). Jesus escaped more than once from the anger of the multitude (see John 8:59; 10:39). God gives wings to the woman to help her escape into the wilderness from the dragon's rage (see Rev. 12:14).

Sometimes God obstructs the power of sin by diverting the thoughts of sin in those who have conceived sin. After Joseph's brothers cast him into a well, passing merchants distracted them. They decided to sell Joseph instead of slaying him (see Gen. 37:24–28). When Saul sought David to kill him, God stirred up the Philistines to invade the land and to divert his intentions (see 1 Sam. 23:27).

By these various means God in His providence obstructs the power of sin. He sovereignly controls sin's eruptions in the world. Today is no different than the past: "Every thought and imagination of the heart of man is evil, and that continually" (Gen. 6:5). It is only by God's mercy that all the land is not full of violence.

It is by the mercy of God that we sleep safely in our beds at night and enjoy the quiet in our lives. For we, our families, and our liberties might all be destroyed a thousand times over but for His mercy. The psalmist says, "My soul is among lions: and I lie even among them that are set on fire, even the sons of men, whose teeth are spears and arrows, and their tongue a sharp sword" (Ps. 57:4). But "God breaks their teeth in their mouths, even the great teeth of the young lions" (Ps. 58:6).

If God obstructs sin in many different ways, in what condition do the wicked find themselves? They are, as we have seen, "like a troubled sea that cannot rest" (Isa. 57:20). Every day God fills them with disappointments in their lusts. David describes them as wandering dogs: "They return at evening: they make a noise like a dog, and go around the city. They belch out with their mouth: swords are in their lips," yet they are not able to accomplish their designs (Ps. 59:6–7). Envy, malice, anger, and revenge devour their hearts in frustration. Lusts never satisfy them.

How should God's people respond to the evil around them? Let them be encouraged to know that God uses even the wrath of man to praise Him (see Ps. 76:10). The remainder of wrath He restrains. Remember also the occasions when you have conceived sin, but God obstructed its commission. Thank God for His mercy that hindered you from falling further into sin. In all these ways we see the magistracy of God, ruling in His provident mercy.

2. God's grace in inward changes diverts the will to sin.

God also aborts the fetus of sin within men. God does this in two ways: by restraining grace and by renewing grace. He does the former to believer and unbeliever alike. He does the latter to believers.

God brings new reasons into the minds of sinners to change their purposes and plans by His *restraining grace.* Let us consider five aspects of the efficacy of the Spirit of God in restraining grace.

First, God stops men in their tracks by showing them the difficulty, if not the impossibility, of what they want to do. Herod wanted to put John the Baptist to death, but he feared the people (see Matt. 14:5). Likewise, the Pharisees would have openly denounced the ministry of Jesus, but they feared the crowd (see Matt. 21:26). Later they were held back from killing Him for the same reason (see 21:46).

Second, God uses the inconveniences and troubles that befall people to stop others in their pursuit of sin. Paul uses this argument in Romans 2:14–15—"For when the Gentiles, which have not the law, do by nature the things contained in the law, these, having not the law, are a law unto themselves: Which shew the work of the law written in their hearts, their conscience also bearing witness, and their thoughts the mean while accusing or else excusing one another." They do not have the law, yet the results of sin persuade them to do what is lawful. Felix trembled at Paul's preaching about the righteousness and judgment to come (see Acts 24:25). Likewise, Job tells us that the judgment of God has a strong influence on men to keep them from sin (see Job 31:1–3).

Third, God makes men see the unprofitableness of the sin they seek to commit. "What profit is it," argued Joseph's brothers, "if we slay our brother, and conceal his blood?" (Gen. 37:26). "We will get nothing from it. It will bring neither advantage nor satisfaction to us," they thought. Likewise, there is nothing good or desirable, either during this life or the next, in pursuing sin for its own sake.

Fourth, God shows the advantages of seeking what is good, honest, comely, praiseworthy, and acceptable to Himself. This is the grand highway for the saints of God to travel when facing temptations and conceptions of sin. The Christian is reminded of the eternal love of God and of its fruits. He is reminded of the cross of Christ, His sufferings, the costliness of His mediation, and the concern of His heart. He is reminded of the love and consolations of the Holy Spirit of which all believers partake. The Christian is also reminded of the beauty and glory of the gospel, of the excellence and comeliness of obedience, of the wounding afresh of the Lord Jesus Christ and putting Him to shame, and of their grieving of the Holy Spirit and defiling His dwelling place in their hearts. God often reminds His people of the benefits of fleeing from sin. We see this in the life of Joseph (see Gen. 39:9) and David (see 1 Sam. 25:29–31).

Fifth, God sometimes works secretly in the hearts of men to restrain them from evil. God told Abimelech, I "have withheld you from sinning against me" (Gen. 20:6). Abimelech thought he acted in integrity, but God alone kept him from sin.

God also worked secretly to change the heart of Esau. He became so angry at his brother Jacob that he sought to kill him (see Gen. 27:41). Jacob himself feared that Esau would also "smite the mother with the children" (Gen. 32:11) and wipe out his entire family. But God's Spirit entered into Esau and effected a radical change in his murderous heart. When they met, Esau fell on the neck of Jacob and embraced him (see Gen. 33:4).

In another instance, Laban pursued Jacob with intent to slay him. In a dream, God intervened and pursuaded him differently. Elihu speaks of a similar experience (see Job 33:15–17).

God also prevents the development of sin by His *renewing grace.* This occurs either with the conversion of the sinner or during the life of the believer.

In the mystery of God's grace and love, He sometimes meets men in the midst of their sinful determinations to change the whole course of their lives. He melts their lusts, He fills them with shame and repentance, and He changes their hearts. God met Paul in this way on the Damascus road. In the midst of the violence of his sin, Paul cried out, "Lord, what would you have me to do?" (Acts 9:6).

Paul later saw his own conversion as a pattern of God's dealings with others. "For this cause I obtained mercy, that in me first Jesus Christ might shew forth all longsuffering, for a pattern to them which should hereafter believe on him to life everlasting" (1 Tim. 1:16). This is the way God often uses to face and change sinners, meeting them at the very point of their scorn and derision of His Word. God met Dionysius the Areopagite in this way (see Acts 17:18–34).

God also renews grace and gives special helps to believers. Asaph says, "My feet were almost gone; my steps had well nigh slipped" (Ps. 73:2). He found himself on the brink of unbelief as he reflected on God's providence in the government of the world. It was then that God stepped in to renew his confidence in Him.

This is the distinctive ministry of Christ, "to succour them that are tempted" (Heb. 2:18). He gives "grace to help in time of need" (Heb. 4:16). Here we see a large part of Christ's care and faithfulness to poor saints. He does not allow the power of sin to overwhelm them or carry them into the ways of the world. He protects them from dishonoring the gospel or negating their witness in the world. Christ steps in with renewing grace to help them. "There hath no temptation taken you but such as is common to man: but God is faithful, who will not suffer you to be tempted above that you are able; but will with the temptation also make a way of escape, that ye may be able to bear it" (1 Cor. 10:13).

In addition to these general ways in which God works on the will of the sinner, either by common convictions or special grace, God uses His own special ways. He often works upon the power and will of sinners by *afflictions.* God sends a sickness or other loss of power to check the headlong course of a sinner, in the midst of the full pursuit of sin. The psalmist confesses, "Before I was afflicted I went astray: but now have I kept thy word" (Ps. 119:67).

We have considered some of the ways God uses to stop the progress of sin both in believers and unbelievers. But if we sought to know all of His ways, we would only realize how small is our knowledge of Him and His ways with us.

THE EFFECTS OF INDWELLING SIN

We have dealt extensively with indwelling sin. Let us now examine more briefly the remaining arguments about this subject and its effects upon us. First, we will examine the invasion of sin into believers' lives and then trace the gradual moral decline of those who have previously trusted in God. Finally, we shall examine the resistance of indwelling sin to the law of God.

THE INVASION OF VIOLENT SIN INTO BELIEVERS' LIVES

We see in Scripture the power of violent sin upon numerous believers. These were not little people, but giants of the faith—men like Noah, Lot, David, Hezekiah, and others who were eminent in their walk with God. These were not people who fell into sin at the beginning of their walk with God, when they could have been excused as novices. Instead, they fell after long experience in the ways of the grace of God.

Noah long walked with God before sin surprised him (see Gen. 9). Righteous Lot appears only to have defiled himself toward the end of his life. David richly experienced the grace of God in close, spiritual communion before sin cast him down. The same may be said of Hezekiah. If sin cast down such experienced men of God, what about us?

It is significant that these men received great and wonderful mercies from the hand of God before sin invaded their lives, but they failed to remain diligent and watchful. God delivered Noah from the great flood. Yet, with the devastated world around him as a reminder of God's grace, he soon fell into drunkenness. After God delivered David out of all his troubles, he fell into adultery and contrived murder. After God delivered Hezekiah from death, he fell into carnal pride and boasting. Even in the midst of God's blessings, no one is safe unless he keeps close to God. He alone is able to keep us.

Can anyone boast that he is better than Noah, who "was a perfect man in his generations and walked with God"? (Gen. 6:9). Are we better than Lot, a "righteous man, vexed with the evil deeds of ungodly men"? (2 Peter 2:7–8). Are we more holy or wise or watchful than David, who was "a man after [God's] own heart"? (1 Sam. 13:14). Are we better than Hezekiah, who reminded God that he had served Him "with a perfect heart"? (Isa. 38:3). Their testimonies float as buoys marking where the sands, Shoals, and rocks of sin left them shipwrecked. Only God in His faithfulness kept them from utter loss and ruin.

THE GRADUAL MORAL DECLINE OF BELIEVERS

Sin sometimes appears to topple strong believers overnight. But sin often causes a gradual decline in zeal and holiness in believers' obedience to—and communion with—God. David declined gradually into sin when he numbered the people (see 2 Sam. 24 and 1 Chron. 21). He would not have done this in his earlier days, when he followed God in the wilderness of temptations and trials. During that time he was full of faith, love, humility, brokenness of heart, zeal, and tender affection for all of God's ordinances. But the deception of sin impaired his strength.

We see this gradual decline in the churches Christ addresses in Revelation 2 and 3. Christ mentions many good things, for example, about the church at Ephesus. Yet He declares, "You have lost your first love. Remember, therefore, from whence you have fallen, and repent, and do the first works" (Rev. 2:4–5).

Scripture is replete with warnings about the dangers of decay. It refers to "the kindness of thy youth" and "the love of thine espousals" (Jer. 2:2), to our "first faith" (1 Tim. 5:12), and to "the beginning of our confidence" (Heb. 3:14). God's Word also warns us to "lose not the things we have wrought" (2 John 8). In light of these warnings, what tests should we continually use to determine the extent of our own decline?

1. Evaluate your zeal for God.

Is our zeal for God what it used to be—warm, living, vigorous, and effective? Or has the abundance of iniquity dulled us and made our hearts cold? Do we still say with the psalmist, "Rivers of water run down mine eyes, because they keep not thy law"? (Ps. 119:136). Are we solicitous about Christ's interest in this world, as Eli was about the ark? Do we still "contend earnestly for the faith once delivered to the saints"? (Jude 3). Do we labor to judge and condemn the world by our holy and separate lifestyle? Has the world ruined our profession and confession of faith? Though we may not like them, we should ask ourselves these salutary questions.

2. Examine your delight in the worship of God.

We could ask ourselves many questions on the subject of worship. How precious is the Word of God to us? What do we still know of the power of the Holy Spirit in our lives? Do we still enjoy the Lord's day as the Lord's day? Is it a real joy to our souls? Do we still converse with the saints of God as our inspiration and model? Or do we say of our Christian lives, "What a weariness it is!" (Mal. 1:13). Are we irked by duties and obligations that we once rejoiced in doing?

3. Inspect your sensitivity to sin.

We can also ask about the concern we have to godly obedience and the sensitivity we have to sinning. Do we still maintain spiritual disciplines? Do we have the same love for the brethren? Do we have the same readiness to take up our cross? Do we have the same humility of mind and the same spirit of self-denial? The fog of sin and lust fills the atmosphere around us, so that we cannot always reply in the affirmative. What is the extent of decline in your own life?

All decline comes from indwelling sin. Decline stands out as evidence of the continuing power of sin. However, when we mourn the reality of sin's power, we can also rejoice in the greater power God gives us to overcome it. What are the sources of this greater power?

One source of God's power comes from His gifts to the body of Christ. They are "for the perfecting of the saints" (Eph. 4:12) to complete the whole work of faith and obedience. They are "for the work of the ministry" to prevent decay and decline. But what if Satan and his instruments work against us in subtleness and deceit? God has designed these gifts for our safeguard and deliverance. As we exercise these gifts, we "grow up in him in all things, who is the head, even Christ" (4:15). God uses them to mature us to fruitfulness.

God also keeps us from forgetting the help He offers us. He multiplies His commands, exhortations, and promises in the Scriptures for this purpose (see Heb. 2:1). God continually challenges us, "Why will you die? Why will you wither and decay? Come to the pastures provided for you, and your soul shall live." When we see believers pining away, getting leaner in their souls, we know it is indwelling sin they must rid themselves of.

In addition to these more outward sources of spiritual growth and power, we also experience those supplies that come continually from the grace of Christ. As our living head, Christ says, "Because I live, ye shall live also" (John 14:19). He continually communicates life to all that are His. In Him is the fountain of life. As a paraphrase of Galatians 2:20, I can say, "The spiritual life that I have is not my own. I did not induce it, and I cannot maintain it. It is only and solely the work of Christ. It is not I who live, but Christ lives in me. My whole life is His alone."

Moreover, Christ does not just give us life, but abundant life—vigorous, strong, flourishing, fruitful life. He came not only that we might have life, but that we might have it "more abundantly" (John 10:10). This involves our corporate life as believers. The whole body is fitted and joined together with the effectual increase of God, making "increase of the body unto the edifying of itself in love" (Eph. 4:16). Christ's treasures of grace are unsearchable, His stores inexhaustible, His life full and eternal. Why then do we not grow and flourish with these resources? It is not for lack of Christ's gracious communication. Rather, it is because of the blockages that lust and sin make within us. That is all!

But with Christ's continual supplies of grace we also have the readiness of Christ to aid us at all times. As a "merciful and faithful high priest ... he is able to succour them that are tempted" (Heb. 2:17–18). On that account, we "come with boldness to the throne of grace, that we may obtain mercy, and find grace to help in time of need" (Heb. 4:16). In other words, we obtain grace seasonable, suitable, and sufficient for every trial and difficulty we face.

Indeed, the Christian has innumerable obligations and means

from the love, commands, and sufficiency of God to press forward toward maturity (see Heb. 6:1). Yet the subtleness and power of sin still haunt and threaten the believer. The most serious threat of sin is its power to cause believers to fall into moral decline before God. Let us watch against this vigilantly, because it comes so gradually.

Many steps lead to the decline of grace in believers. Many fresh springs of grace open up to new converts, refreshing them with desires for God in faith, love, holiness, fruitfulness, and obedience. But if they neglect these springs, decay sets in. The fresh, vigorous sense of pardoning mercy disappears. If they maintain a deep sense of this mercy, however, their life as a believer will be empowered. Jesus said of the poor woman who came to Him in Luke 7:47, "To whom much has been forgiven, the same loves much." A great sense of God's forgiveness generates much love for the Lord.

The fresh taste of spiritual things keeps Christians from worldly contentments. Having tasted the wine of the gospel, they realize this is the best. Jesus once asked the disciples if they would go away. "Lord," they replied, "to whom shall we go? thou hast the words of eternal life" (John 6:68). Like a prisoner long kept in a dungeon, then brought into the sudden light of sunshine, the new glory transcends all other experiences.

In this new state of forgiveness and joy in Christ, the convert cannot do enough for God. His zeal for Christ sometimes leads him to acts of impudence. But the processes of decay begin with the tainting of these fresh springs.

The first contaminant is *the development of sloth and negligence of God's grace.* Unless obedience and diligence keep open the well of salvation, it becomes clogged, as the Philistines stopped up the wells of the Israelites. This occurs when indwelling sin clogs the soul with careless indifference to the former apprehensions of divine love and with moral negligence to the continuing thoughts of faith. God often complains that His people have "forgotten the God of [their] salvation" (Isa. 17:10).

The second corrupting influence is the *loss of reverence for God.* The disposition of the soul loses its attitude of reverence and awe of God. The apostle cautions us in dealing with God to use reverence and godly fear, because of His purity, holiness, and majesty (see Heb. 12:28–29). The Lord said this about the destruction of Nadab and Abihu: "I will be sanctified in them that come near me" (Lev. 10:3).

We must relate to God with reverence in a holy manner. When people begin to slight Him and act irreverently toward Him, they lose a sense of God's greatness. Hezekiah sinned because he "rendered not according to the benefits done to him" (2 Chron. 32:25).

We must keep close to God—beholding His glory—if we are to be "changed into the same image" (2 Cor. 3:18). But when we lose our reverence for God, we become less like God. We lose the power of holiness and no longer walk close to Him. Some talk about God and spiritual things as much as they ever did before, but they have lost His power in their lives. Remain serious about spiritual things if you want God's blessing in your life.

The third pollutant is the *loss of the simplicity of the gospel.* Foolish and speculative opinions corrupt the simplicity of the gospel. Vain speculations are the work of the flesh. Paul expressed jealousy for his Corinthian converts, lest their minds "should by any means be corrupted from the simplicity that is in Christ" (2 Cor. 11:3). He knew that this pollutant would diminish their faith, love, and obedience.

Unfortunately, we see the same thing happening today. After walking with the Lord for many years, some believers listen to the vain opinions of men, then despise their own experiences of grace. They reject all the efficacy of the truth. John warns the elect lady and her children to take heed lest they should lose the things that they had wrought (see 2 John 8). There is nothing with which we need to use more vigilance than to see that we do not lose the efficacy of God's Word within our lives. We need to keep fresh the power of God's Word in our souls.

The fourth corrupting influence is *the lack of vigilance against Satan.* When Christ first comes to possess our hearts, Satan retreats dispossessed and frustrated. Like his first fruitless attempts with our Lord, he leaves "for a season" (Luke 4:13). But he returns as soon as he has the advantage to entangle the believer.

Picture a kind man who seeks to do good things for his neighbors. If unscrupulous men entangle him in a legal case, he suddenly finds himself so preoccupied with his legal affairs that he can no longer do anything else. In the same way, Satan seeks to entrap a believer with indwelling sin, whenever he sees a weakness that he can exploit to his own advantage. Peter warns, "Be sober and vigilant." Why? "Because [of] your adversary the devil" (1 Peter 5:8).

The fifth impurity is *the imitation of the poor example of professing Christians.* Indwelling sin takes advantage of the bad example of professing Christians. When people first become believers, they have an enthusiastic and even reverent attitude toward those they believe are further along the road as Christians. Then they find out the truth when they see them act crookedly and inconsistently—indeed, not unlike the people in the world. Gradually, they begin to imitate these professors, thinking they can also sin and apparently flourish.

This tragedy occurs because young Christians do not recognize the peculiar weaknesses of professing Christians. Instead, these weaknesses appear to be the norm. Beware, for many professing Christians are sick and wounded and not to be imitated. They are not good models. Moreover, the real character of true Christians often lies beneath the surface. The obvious is often all show, while true integrity remains quietly hidden.

The sixth pollutant is *the enjoyment of some secret lust in the heart.* This is something the believer may have to struggle against, yet can only do so very weakly. When some lust lodges within our heart, a habitual decline in holiness follows. In his early days, David kept his heart close to God. He could say, "I was upright before him, and I kept myself from iniquity" (Ps. 18:23). Likewise, Paul could "keep his body in subjection" (1 Cor. 9:27). But once sin enters the heart, it weakens one's spiritual strength.

Secret lusts sap one's confidence in God and hinder the exercise of faith and prayer, so that the soul cannot "look up" (Ps. 40:12). It darkens the mind. It breaks out at times into scandalous sins. It seizes the soul like a virulent disease. It is so malignant that eventually the soul can scarcely keep alive at all.

The seventh contaminant is *the negligence of private communion with God.* We have already seen how indwelling sin deceives in turning the mind's attention away from the practice of prayer and meditation. When it succeeds and prevails, habitual prayerlessness may result. God complains, "You have not called upon me; you have been weary of me" (Isa. 43:22). Neglect of prayer proceeds from weariness and withdrawal from God. A believer in this state is like a dying tree. Because the roots have been killed, all the leaves will eventually wither.

Our Lord points out the importance of praying in secret, where only the eyes of God can see (see Matt. 6:6). No ulterior motives affect a man when he seeks to enjoy God's presence and grace in secret. When indwelling sin cuts a person off from diligent and constant communion with God, then a decline of the whole person's obedience will inevitably follow.

The eighth impurity is *the increase of knowledge without answerable practice.* The apostle tells us, "Knowledge puffs up" (1 Cor. 8:1). Theoretical knowledge swells to undue proportions, like a man with dropsy, or like a plant with much greenery but no fruit. When believers view evangelical truths as mere head knowledge, they become empty and barren. Those who were once humble and walked closely with God become mere talkers. Their empty knowledge becomes food for sin. It produces vanity in the mind without any rebuke from the conscience.

When Christians enjoy merely talking, writing, and studying about religion, their conscience becomes pacified (see Ezek. 33:32). It lodges no protest in the soul. Thus men content themselves with notions of truth, without laboring to experience the power of truth in their hearts. They bring forth no fruit in their lives. Decay ensues.

The ninth corrupting influence is *the growth in worldly wisdom.* This is similar to what we have just said. The prophet charged: "Your wisdom and your knowledge have perverted you" (Isa. 47:10). True wisdom consists of trusting God. The world's wisdom says to trust yourself. It works to destroy all faith and causes the soul to enter into self-deception. How many simple believers stumble over the example of the worldly wise, who falsely led them away. Some believers are never the same again.

The tenth pollutant is *the failure to repent of some great sin.* David kept such a sin because he wanted to keep his reputation. But great sins cause great changes in the life of a believer. David complained, "My wounds stink and are corrupt because of my foolishness" (Ps. 38:5). Unless a broken bone is set well, a person becomes a cripple for life. Likewise, without repentance, a person never fully heals. Sin only hardens and decays his soul.

[In his next chapter, Owen deals summarily with indwelling sin in unregenerate man, although he admits it is not relevant to the theme of his treatise. For this reason, we have taken the liberty to omit that chapter.]

THE RESISTANCE OF INDWELLING SIN TO THE LAW

We see the strength of sin to produce moral decline in its resistance to the power of the law. We may note several things about this.

1. The law discovers sin.
Like a reagent, sin in the soul reacts in the presence of the law. Paul admits: "I had not known sin, but by the law: for I had not known lust, except the law had said, Thou shalt not covet" (Rom. 7:7). Lust in this sense is a habitual inclination to sin, which only the law exposes.

2. The law recognizes the danger of sin.
Further in the same passage, Paul comments, "Was then that which is good [the law] made death unto me? God forbid. But sin, that it might appear sin, working death in me by that which is good; that sin by the commandment might become exceeding sinful" (Rom. 7:13). Not only does sin "appear" by the law, but it is shown to be "exceeding sinful." It is not a minor affair, but deadly and mortal, because it produces alienation from God.

3. The law judges the sinner.
It lets him plainly know what he should expect. The law's proper work is to expose sin in order to judge it. Yet its judgment is a merciful warning, showing that if one persists in sin, the consequences are clearly spelled out. This leaves the soul without excuse.

4. The law disturbs the heart.

The effect of its judgment disturbs and frightens the soul, so that it cannot enjoy or rest in its sinful companionship. Like a poor beast that has a deadly arrow in its flank, it is utterly miserable wherever it goes.

5. The law slays the soul.

Eventually, the law so disturbs the soul that, depriving it of self-righteousness and any hope, it destroys the soul. It leaves it as a poor, helpless, hopeless creature that is "dead in trespasses and sins" (Eph 2:1). Another verse declares, "I was alive without the law once: but when the commandment came, sin revived, and I died" (Rom. 7:9).

Yet this death is still not death to indwelling sin. The law cannot deprive sin of its dominion and power. As Paul argues in Romans 7, he who is under the law is also under sin. In other words, whatever power a man's conscience may exert against sin, he is still under sin's dominion. The law only intensifies the misery and bondage that a sinner feels. It simply adds to his complexity and terror. Like the Israelites under Pharaoh, the law leaves a man "in a very evil case" (Exod. 5:19). Indeed, the law enrages sin, provoking it to react all the more violently.

It is not that we decry the significance of the law. God has established it for a purpose. But the subduing of sin is not its task. God did not design the law for that purpose. It is no dishonor if the law cannot do that which is not its proper task (Rom. 8:3). Thus we experience the faithful, constant preaching of the Word against sin in a church congregation for years on end. Yet we see no real effect of this on the lives of its members. These congregations actually proclaim the power of sin over the dispensation of the law! It is not the letter of the law but the efficacy of the spirit of God that truly matters.

We also see the power of sin in the strenuous efforts of men—ignorant of the righteousness that is in Christ—to live upright lives. They become ashamed of the guilt of sin and endeavor to abstain from it. They promise by vows to deal with besetting sins, and for a space of time they appear to succeed. But they find it is only a temporary release before they fall back into their old sinful habits. At best, they can only hope to restrain some of the more obvious public evidences of sin. But inwardly, they continue to toil under the burden and perplexity of sin.

True gospel grace, however, charges those beasts within us that seem untamable and fierce and changes them. The prophet anticipates this when he describes the wolf acting as a kid, or the lion as a lamb, or the bear as a cow. When this happens, "a little child shall lead them" (Isa. 11:6). Locking up wild beasts does not change them, for the inward violence remains. Likewise, it is grace alone that changes the heart of man.

Yet men continue to persist in extraordinary means of mortification by pilgrimages, penances, and self-torture, as well as by prayers, fastings, and the cloistered life. Without God's grace, they persist in these self-invented ways while remaining ignorant of the true righteousness of God.

What do these men achieve by their efforts? Paul says they do not attain the righteousness sought; they do not conform to the law; and they do not mortify sin, or even weaken it (Rom. 9:31–32). What sin loses sensually, it gains spiritually in blindness, superstition, self-righteousness, and pride. These efforts of men lead to contempt of gospel righteousness, and so sin reigns in them no less than in the most profligate sinners of the world.

What then is the purpose of mortification? We have not written this to make Christians despair, but to help them discover the power, deceit, prevalence, and success of this great adversary of our souls—namely, indwelling sin. Our response must be that of humility, self-abasement, watchfulness, diligence, and petition to the Lord Christ for relief. As to what concerns the actual mortification of indwelling sin, I recommend to the reader another small treatise for his instruction. [John Owen had written this treatise several years earlier. It is included as the third part of this volume.]

PART II

TEMPTATION OF BELIEVERS

*"Because thou hast kept the
word of my patience,
I also will keep thee from the
hour of temptation,
which shall come upon all the world,
to try them that dwell upon the earth."*
Revelation 3:10

THE NATURE OF
TEMPTATION

If you have noticed the diverse, intense, and varied forms of temptation that confront Christians in these days, then you will understand why I am writing this treatise. Others have urged me to do so. But I myself am also convinced of the seriousness of this danger of ruin to many. As I have experienced temptation myself and have taken stock of the experiences of others, I have had many opportunities to observe human nature and its susceptibility to temptation in its many forms. Because of this, I feel a sense of responsibility to alert others to temptation's dangers and tendencies.

I am not writing for those who live indifferent or blind to the reality of temptation. Nor do I think they can judge what I have written here. Rather, I am writing to those who know our times and the strife and divisions that exist among Christian believers. I write to those who recognize the apostasy, the decline in love, and the overthrow of faith such as former ages never knew.

Indeed, it is in the midst of an obvious decline in reformed faith, personal holiness, and zeal for Christ that I write. Those who already have been seized in "the hour of temptation" are already so captivated by the ways of the world and its lusts that they are too blind to appreciate such a study as this. So I write for those who mourn over our times and who fight to combat the tide of evil that would overwhelm us.

May our faithful and merciful High Priest—who both suffered and touched the feeling of our infirmities—inspire this meditation, for the aid of His servants (see Heb. 4:15). This is my prayer.

ALL BELIEVERS FACE TEMPTATION

"Watch and pray, that ye enter not into temptation" (Matt. 26:41; Mark 14:38; Luke 22:46).

Such vigilance should characterize those in grave danger. The writer of Proverbs 23:34 tells us some "lie down on the top of a mast in the midst of the sea." That is to say, they are men lulled by security while in the midst of potential destruction. The disciples acted like such men while they were with our Savior in the Garden of Gethsemane. A short distance from them their Master offered up "prayers and supplications with strong crying and tears" (Heb. 5:7). Nearby the Jews approached, armed for His and their destruction.

Our Savior had warned the disciples that He would be betrayed that night and be delivered up and slain. Now they saw that He was "sorrowful and very heavy" (Matt. 26:37). Indeed, He told them plainly that His soul was "exceeding sorrowful, even unto death" (26:38). Therefore, He entreated them to watch and pray before He died on their behalf.

Yet in these circumstances, as if they had forsaken their love for Him, they fall fast asleep! This suggests that even the best of saints, when left to themselves, quickly appear to be less than men. For all our own strength is but weakness and our wisdom but folly.

Peter is an example of this weakness. Earlier that night he confidently asserted that, though all should forsake Christ, he would never do so. Now our Savior expostulates with him, saying, "What, could you not watch with me one hour?" (Matt. 26:40). It is as if He is saying, "Are you the same Peter who made such a boast never to forsake me? Yet now you cannot even stay awake to watch for one hour. Is this, then, your dying for me, lying there in your own security, while I am dying for you?"

We find this same root of treachery in our own hearts, and Romans 7:18 describes its fruit. In this situation we are all admonished to realize our condition, weakness, and danger by our Savior's words: "Arise, watch, and pray." I shall not dwell on the specific context of these words for the disciples. Instead, this text contains a general command to all the disciples of Christ throughout all generations. Two aspects of this text will be considered here: first, the evil cautioned against—temptation; and second, the means of its prevalence—our entrance into it (chapter 8).

HOW GOD "TEMPTS" BELIEVERS

I do not intend to talk merely about the nature of temptation in this treatise. We will consider how to avoid temptation in later chapters. Nevertheless, we need to say a few things about the character of temptation first.

Generally speaking, temptation merely means to test, to prove, or to experiment with. In this sense, God sometimes tempts men. Scripture also commands us to test (or tempt) ourselves. That is to say, it is our duty to search ourselves, to try and test ourselves, to know what is in us, and to pray that God will do the same. In this sense, temptation is like a knife that can either cut a man's foot or cut his throat. It may become food or poison, man's exercise or man's destruction.

When we speak of God "tempting," two things merit our

consideration. First, God tempts man to *show him what is in man*, either of grace or of corruption. Because grace and corruption both lie deep within a man's heart, men often deceive themselves in search for one or the other. When we look to see what grace lies in our hearts, evil comes forth. When we look to see what evil abides there, grace appears. Thus the soul remains in uncertainty, and we fail in our tests.

God alone can plumb the depths of our souls. His instruments are His trials. They penetrate the inmost parts of the soul and permit a man to see what lies there. God tempted Abraham to show him his faith. Abraham did not know the power and vigor of his faith until God tested it by a great trial (see Gen. 22:1–2). Likewise, God tested Hezekiah to expose his pride. God left him temporarily to show him what was in his heart (see 2 Chron. 32:31). Hezekiah never realized he had such a proud heart until God tried him and allowed him to see all the filth that poured out from it.

Second, God tests us to *show Himself to man*. God does this for two reasons. In the first place, God's tests help man to realize that He goes ahead of us in grace. Until we face temptation, we think we live by our own strength. We boast that, though others may do this or that evil, we never do it. But when the trial comes, we quickly see where we are kept and where we fall. This is illustrated by Abimelech, who thought he maintained his own personal integrity. In a dream, God showed him, "It was I who kept you from sinning" (Gen. 20:6).

God tests us, as well, to show that He renews grace on our behalf. God continued to test Paul after he prayed for deliverance to reveal to him the sufficiency of His grace (see 2 Cor. 12:9). The sufficiency of His grace does not appear to us until we compare our weakness with the strength of a test. It is like the power of an antidote, which is only revealed after a poison has been

THE NATURE OF TEMPTATION

taken. The precious value of medicine is likewise known only by disease. Similarly, we shall never know the strength of God's grace until we experience temptation.

God accomplishes this revelation of Himself through temptation in three ways. First, God puts upon men *heavy responsibilities and duties* which they consider impossible to undertake and accomplish. God tempted Abraham in this way to sacrifice his own son. Such a challenge seems absurd to reason. It is beyond one's natural instincts. It is grievous, whatever way you look at it. Yet many of us do not know what is in us, or rather what is available to us, until we face such a test.

These tests seem utterly beyond our strength. Yet the duties God requires of us are not in proportion to the strength we possess in ourselves. Rather, they are proportional to the resources available to us in Christ. We do not have the ability in ourselves to accomplish the least of God's tasks. This is a law of grace. When we recognize it is impossible for us to perform a duty in our own strength, we will discover the secret of its accomplishment. But alas, this is a secret we often fail to discover. In the yoke of Christ, it appears rather as a trial or temptation.

Second, God reveals Himself by *great sufferings.* How many have found unexpected strength to endure hardships for Christ and even to die for His sake. Through a trial God called them to experience His strength. Peter says the power of God keeps us, even though we are brought into trying temptations (see 1 Peter 1:5–7). Our temptations, which arise from the "fiery trial" of suffering, ultimately become the trial of our faith.

Third, God reveals Himself *by His providential disposition.* Deuteronomy 13:3 instructs the people not to listen to a false prophet who urges them to go after false gods because "the LORD your God is testing you, to know whether you love the LORD your God with all your heart and with all your soul." Because

God cared for His people, He gave them this warning to guide them away from occasions to sin.

How Satan Tempts Believers

Specifically, temptation means any action that leads to evil. Passively, we sometimes fall into temptation by suffering or affliction. This is the meaning of James 1:2: "Count it all joy when you fall into temptation." We fall into it, not in the sense of actively indulging in evil, but when it afflicts us.

Actively, Satan leads us into evil. In this specific sense, God tempts no man (see James 1:13). He only tests, as He tempted Abraham (see Gen. 22:1), or as He proved the false prophets (see Deut. 13:3). Properly speaking, God does not tempt us to sin.

In the specific sense of the word, temptation denotes *an active efficiency toward sinning.* It is evil breeding evil. Temptation of this sort may come from Satan, from the world, from other men in the world, from ourselves, or from various combinations of these sources.

First of all, Satan sometimes *tempts by himself* without taking advantage of the world, the things or persons in it, or ourselves. He injects evil and blasphemous thoughts into the hearts of God's saints. Satan does this directly, on his own, so he alone will bear the punishment. He forges these fiery darts, with which he attacks us, by his own malice, and they will return with all their poison and venom back into his own heart forever.

Second, Satan often *makes use of the world,* joining forces against us. Thus he tempted our Savior by showing Him "all the kingdoms of the world, and the glory of them" (Matt. 4:8). The variety of the aids Satan finds in the world—both in persons and in things—goes beyond description because of its diversity.

Third, Satan sometimes *takes assistance from us.* We differ from Christ, who the apostle declared "had nothing in [Him]" of sin (John 14:30). Our own desires lure and entice us (see James 1:14). "Desire, when it is conceived, gives birth to sin; *and* sin, when it is full-grown, brings forth death" (1:15). Notice how desire and sin work together. Satan tempted Judas, for example, while Judas himself worked. Satan put it into his heart to betray Christ and entered into him for that purpose (see Luke 22:3). Satan also set the things of the world to work, providing "thirty pieces of silver" for Judas (Matt. 26:15). As well, men were at work; for "they covenanted to give him money" (Luke 22:5). These priests and Pharisees took advantage of Judas' own corruption, for "he was a thief, and had the bag" (John 12:6).

I could also show how the world and our own corruptions act singly by themselves, or jointly in cooperation with Satan and one another, in this business of temptation. However, the principles, ways, and means of temptation, as well as their varied kinds, degrees, efficacies, and causes, defy exhaustive description. We will discover the significance of this later.

CHAPTER 8

ENTERING INTO TEMPTATION

Having seen what temptation means, let us now examine what it means to "*enter* into temptation" (Mark 14:38). First, let us look at three things with which it is often confused. Then we will examine the circumstances of entering into temptation.

WHAT IT IS NOT

First, to enter into temptation is not merely to face temptation. It is impossible for us to be so free of temptation that we never experience it. As long as Satan continues with his power and malice, and as long as the world and its lusts exist around us, we will face temptation. Someone has said, "Christ was made like unto us, that He might be tempted; and we are tempted that we may be made like unto Christ."

Temptation remains a comprehensive reality throughout our whole spiritual warfare. "You are those," says Christ, "who have continued with me in my trials" (Luke 22:28). Since we have no promise that we shall not experience temptation, we should not pray for absolute freedom from temptations. Rather, we should pray, "Lead us not into temptation" (Matt. 6:13). That is to say, we should pray against entering into temptation. We may encounter temptation without entering into it.

Second, to enter into temptation refers to more than the

ordinary work of Satan and our own lust. These are sure to tempt us all the time. But entering into temptation goes beyond the saint's daily experience. It suggests something that leads specifically to the seduction of sin, either by attraction or by fear.

Third, it does not imply being conquered by a temptation. It does not mean that we commit specific sin or evil that tempts us or neglect the duties that we know we must fulfill. A man may enter into temptation and yet not fall under temptation, for God makes a way of escape. When temptation ensnares a man, God treads down Satan and makes the man more than a conqueror, even though he has entered into temptation.

To "fall into temptation," as the apostle describes it in 1 Timothy 6:9, suggests a man falling into a pit. He is not yet killed, but he is caught. He does not have liberty or the knowledge he needs to seek freedom. In 1 Corinthians 10:13 it says, "No temptation has overtaken you that is not common to man." That is to say, temptation never entangles you to such a degree that no way of escape remains. The apostle Peter assures us, "The Lord knoweth how to deliver the godly out of temptations" (2 Peter 2:9). When we become ensnared, God knows how to rescue us. Thus, when we suffer the entanglements of temptation, we enter into temptation.

As long as temptation merely knocks outside the door, we remain free. But when it enters and parleys with the heart, reasons with the mind, and entices and allures the affections— either for a short or a long time, whether the soul is conscious of it or not—then we enter into temptation.

THE CIRCUMSTANCES OF ENTERING INTO TEMPTATION

Entering into temptation requires a number of circumstances. First, it requires that Satan become more earnest than usual. He takes advantage of fears, enticements, persecutions, and seductions from within oneself or from other people. Satan also uses different forms of corruption, lust, fear, trouble, and success to occasion specific forms of temptation.

Second, the heart—though not so involved that it does not dispute or argue in its own defense—is unable to escape the trap of temptation. It is not able to remove the poison injected into it. The soul is often taken off its guard, surprised and trapped in such a way that temptation is not easily avoided. Even though, like the apostle Paul, the soul cries and beseeches the Lord "three times" for the departure of the trial, the entanglement continues (2 Cor. 12:8–9). Usually this entanglement occurs in one of two situations.

The first arises when God (for ends best known to Himself) allows Satan to take peculiar advantage of a man. God allowed Satan to test Job and Peter in this manner.

The second arises when a man's lusts and weaknesses meet with peculiarly provoking objects or occasions. Depending on the specific condition of life he finds himself in, he will enter into temptation. For David, this occurred when he stayed home from battle.

Such a time is called "the hour of temptation" (Rev. 3: 10). It is the season when temptation comes to a head. Indeed, every great and pressing temptation has its own hour or season when it becomes most active, operative, and prevalent. It may take a long time to come, but it comes in its own time. Hence that temptation that possesses little or no power over a man in normal circumstances suddenly takes on an overpowering reality. Either this occurs because it now assumes new powers and effectiveness or the person weakens before encountering it.

David in his youth probably had been tempted to commit adultery or murder, but the hour of temptation had not reached its full power in advantage over him—and he had escaped. But when it came to a head, as it did when he saw Bathsheba, David was caught. The first lesson to learn is this: Be prepared for the time when temptation becomes strong.

To learn this lesson, we need to discover how temptation reaches its "hour." This it does in various ways. First, it does so by urgings over a long period of time, so that the mind becomes accustomed to the evil thought. At first temptation may shock the soul by its ugly appearance. The soul cries out, "Am I a dog to feel like this?" Unless this disgust deepens daily, the soul gradually grows accustomed to temptation's familiarity and finally asks, "This is just a peccadillo, is it not?" Temptation takes the soul off guard and reaches its climax. Lust then entices and traps the soul. As James 1:15 describes it, sin is "conceived."

Second, when sin prevails over other people, and the soul does not react with disgust and abhorrence, then temptation takes advantage of us as well. It is crucial that we learn from the fall of others to be prepared ourselves. When sin prevails against others, its hour may also come to us. We read in 2 Timothy 2:17–18 that the fall of Hymeneus and Philetus led to "the overthrow of the faith of some."

Third, sin sometimes associates itself with other considerations that are not evil in themselves. The temptation of the Galatians to fall from the purity of the gospel took advantage of their natural desire to escape persecution and to enjoy consensus with the Jews. By pleading for good things, they unwittingly gave life to temptation itself.

If temptation uses these ways to reach its "hour," we must ask, "How will we know when temptation reaches its peak?" There are two ways to discern this. The first is by temptation's restless urgency. When it is time for battle, temptation gives the soul no rest. Satan sees his advantage, appraises the forces that he can deploy, and knows in this moment he must prevail or lose. If Satan does not seize this opportune time, he will miss his chance.

When he had things ready against Christ, Satan made it "the hour of darkness" (Luke 22:53). When temptation discovers a thousand darknesses and presses within the doors of the mind or knocks outside (by soliciting, taking advantage, and seizing opportunities), let the soul recognize the time of his trial has come. It is the time to "stand still, and see the salvation of the LORD" (Exod. 14:13).

The second way we know the time has come is by the union of fears and allurements. When both come together, we know it is the hour of temptation. This was true in David's case with the murder of Uriah. On the one hand, he feared Uriah's revenge against Bathsheba (and possibly against himself), as well as the exposure of his sin. On the other hand, David remained allured by his present enjoyment with Bathsheba, for whom he lusted. Sin sometimes carries men away by their love for sin, and they continue in it because they fear what will ensue if they stop. When these two forces unite—sometimes enticing, sometimes frightening us—then the reasons between them become confused in our minds. Sin entangles us and the hour of temptation comes.

This then is what it means to "enter into temptation." This is also the "hour" of its arrival.

CHAPTER 9

THE POWER OF TEMPTATION

It is the great duty of all believers not to enter into temptation. God indeed is able to "deliver the godly out of temptations" (2 Peter 2:9). Yet it is our great task to use all diligence so that we do not fall into temptation. Our Savior expresses His concern for His disciples by teaching them to pray, "Lead us not into temptation" (Matt. 6:13). Since our Lord knows the power of temptation, having experienced it, He knows how vulnerable we are to it (see Heb. 2:18). He rewards our obedience by keeping us "in the hour of temptation" (Rev. 3:10).

Let us learn more about the power of temptation in order to avoid it. Since temptation brings out many basic issues, Scripture has much to say about it. In the parable of the sower, Christ compares the seed sown on the rocky, thin soil to those who, "when they hear, receive the word with joy, but have no root, for they only believe for a while" (Luke 8:13). The preaching of the Word affects them. They believe. They make a profession. They bring forth some fruit. But how long do they continue? Christ says, "In time of temptation they fall away" (Luke 8:13). Once tempted, they are gone forever.

Likewise, in Matthew 7:26, Jesus speaks of the parable of the "foolish man, who built his house upon the sand." But what happens to this house of professed faith? It shelters its occupant, it keeps him warm, and it stands for a while. But when the rain descends (that is to say, when temptation comes), it falls utterly, and its fall is great. This foolish man is like Judas, who followed our Savior three years. All went well for a time. But he no sooner entered into temptation—when Satan winnowed him—than he was lost. Demas preached the gospel until the love of the world entered into his soul, and then he turned utterly aside as well.

Among the saints of God, we see the solemn power of temptation. Take Adam, "the son of God," created in the image of God, full of integrity, righteousness, and holiness (Luke 3:38). He possessed a far greater inherent stock of ability than we have, since he had never been enticed or seduced. Yet no sooner did Adam enter into temptation but he was undone, lost, and ruined, and all his posterity with him. What should we expect then, when in our temptations we must deal not only with a cunning devil, but also with a cursed world and a corrupt heart?

Abraham is called the father of the faithful, for it is his faith that is recommended as the pattern to all who believe (see Rom. 4:11–17). Yet twice he entered into the same temptation (namely, his fear about his wife). Twice he committed sin. He dishonored God, and no doubt his soul lost its peace (see Gen. 12 and 20).

David is called "a man after [God's] own heart" (1 Sam. 13:14). Yet what a dreadful story we read of his immorality! No sooner did temptation entangle him than he plunged into adultery. Seeking deliverance by his own devices, he became all the more entangled until he lay as one dead under the power of sin and folly.

We should also mention Noah, Lot, Hezekiah, and Peter, whose temptations and falls God recorded for our own instruction. Like the inhabitants of Samaria who received the letter of Jehu, we should ask, "If two kings were not able to stand before him, how then shall we stand?" (2 Kings 10:4). For this reason the apostle urges us to exercise tenderness toward those who fall into sin. Paul writes, "Consider yourselves, lest you also be tempted" (Gal. 6:1). Seeing the power of temptation in others, let us beware, for we do not know when or how we also may be tempted. What folly it is that many should be so blind and bold, after all these and other warnings, to put themselves before temptation.

We need to examine ourselves to see our own weaknesses and to note the power and efficacy of temptation. In ourselves, we are weakness itself. We have no strength, no power to withstand. Self-confidence produces a large part of our weakness, as it did with Peter. He who boasts that he can do anything can in fact do nothing as he should. This is the worst form of weakness, similar to treachery. However strong a castle may be, if a treacherous party resides inside (ready to betray at the first opportunity possible), the castle cannot be kept safe from the enemy. Traitors occupy our own hearts, ready to side with every temptation and to surrender to them all.

Do not flatter yourself that you can hold out against temptation's power. Secret lusts lie lurking in your own heart that will never give up until they are either destroyed or satisfied. "Am I a dog, that I should do this thing?" asks Hazael (2 Kings 8:13). Yes, you will be such a dog, if you are like the king of Syria. Temptation and self-interest will dehumanize you. In theory we abhor lustful thoughts, but once temptation enters our heart, all contrary reasonings are overcome and silenced.

INADEQUATE SAFEGUARDS AGAINST THE POWER OF TEMPTATION

To be safe from such danger, we need to examine our own hearts. A man's heart is his true self. If a man is not a believer, but only a professor of the gospel, what will his heart do? Proverbs 10:20

says, "The heart of the wicked is of little worth." While outwardly it appears to have value, inwardly it is worthless. Because the sphere of temptation lies in the heart, an unbeliever cannot resist it when it comes like a flood.

No one, indeed, should trust his own heart. Proverbs 28:26 says, "He that trusteth in his own heart is a fool." Peter did this when he boasted, "Although all shall forsake thee, I will not" (Mark 14:29). This was his folly, his self-confidence. The heart of a man makes such wonderful promises before temptation comes. But "the heart is deceitful" (Jer. 17:9). Indeed, it is "deceitful above all things." It has a thousand shifts and treacheries, and when trial comes, temptation steals it away just as "wine and new wine take away understanding" (Hos. 4:11).

We need then to examine some of the inadequate measures we often use in our attempts to safeguard the heart in the hour of temptation.

1. The love of honor in the world.

By one's walk and profession one obtains reputation and esteem in the church. So some argue, "Can I afford to lose such a reputation in the church of God by giving way to this lust, or to that temptation, or in dealing in this or that public evil?" This seems so strong an argument that many use it as a shield against any assaults that come. They would rather die a thousand deaths than lose their reputation in the church.

But what about "the third part of the stars of heaven"? (Rev. 12:4). Did they not shine in the firmament? Were they not fully aware of their honor, stature, usefulness, and reputation? Yet when the dragon comes with his temptations, he casts them down to the earth. Those who have no better defenses than the love of honor are inadequately equipped to deal with temptation. Sadly, it is possible for those with great reputations to suffer destruction when their only defense lies in their own good name. If this does not keep the stars of heaven, how do you think it will keep you?

2. The fear of shame and reproach.

Not for all the world would some people bring upon themselves the shame and reproach associated with certain temptations. Their concern, however, tends to focus only upon open sins, such as the world notices and abhors. This motive proves useless when dealing with sins of conscience or with sins of the heart. Innumerable excuses are offered to the heart when one relies on this as the predominant defense against temptation.

3. The desire not to disturb one's peace of mind, wound one's conscience, or risk the danger of hellfire.

One might think that this would act as a major safeguard to preserve people in the hour of temptation. Indeed, we should use this as a major defense, for nothing is more important than striving to maintain our peace with God. Yet several reasons indicate this motive alone is not effective.

The peace of some only provides a false sense of security made up of presumptions and false hopes. Even believers cling to this. David enjoyed this false peace until Nathan came to see him. Laodicea rested in it while on the verge of destruction. The church of Sardis also claimed this peace while she lay dying. It is only true peace in Christ that keeps us, and nothing else. Nothing that God will not preserve in the last day keeps us now. False peace acts as a broken reed, piercing the hand that leans upon it.

Even the true peace we desire to safeguard our soul may prove useless as a defense in the hour of temptation. Why? Because we are so vulnerable to excuses. "This evil is so trivial," we say. Or we argue that it is so questionable. Or we argue that it does not openly and flagrantly offend the conscience. We rationalize with such excuses while maintaining our own peace of mind. We even rationalize that others of God's people have fallen, yet kept their peace and recovered from it. Facing a thousand such arguments—set up like batteries of guns against a fort—the soul finally surrenders.

If we only focus on the one safeguard of peace, the enemy will assault us elsewhere. True, it is one piece of armor for our protection, but we are commanded to "put on the *whole* armour of God" (Eph. 6:11). If we depend upon this one element of defense, temptation will enter and prevail in twenty other ways.

A man, for example, may be tempted to worldliness, unjust gain, revenge, vanity, and many other things. If he focuses his attention on this one safeguard of peace and considers himself safe, he will neglect other needs. He may neglect his private communion with God or overlook his tendency to be sensual. In the end he may not be one whit better than if he had succumbed to the temptation that most obviously harassed him. Experience shows that this peace of mind fails, therefore, as a safeguard. There is no saint of God who does not value the peace he enjoys. Yet how many fail in the day of temptation!

4. The thought of the vileness of sinning against God.

How could we do this thing, when to sin against God is to do so against His mercies and to wound Jesus Christ, who died for us? Unfortunately, we see every day that even this is not a sure and infallible defense. No such defense exists.

Why do these motives fail us in the hour of temptation? Their sources betray their inadequacy. For they arise either from the universal and habitual disposition of our heart or from the temptation itself. We should remain wary of such counselors.

THE POWER OF TEMPTATION

It is helpful to consider the power of temptation in the light of what we have just said. The power of temptation is to darken the mind, so that a person becomes unable to make right judgments about things as he did before entering into temptation. The god of this world blinds men's minds so that they do not see the glory of Christ in the gospel (see 2 Cor. 4:4). Likewise, the very nature of every temptation darkens the heart of the person who becomes tempted. This occurs in various ways.

First, the imagination and thought can be so obsessed with some object that the mind is distracted from those things that could relieve and help it. Someone might be tempted to believe that God has forsaken him, or God hates him, so that he expresses no interest in Christ. He becomes so depressed that he feels none of the remedies suggested to him will help. Meanwhile, he becomes obsessed with the temptation that fixates him.

Temptation also darkens the mind by the tragic confusion of the inclinations of the heart. Look around you and see how readily temptation entangles people's feelings. Show me someone not occupied with hope, love, and fear (of what he should not do), and I will quickly point out his blindness. His present judgment of things will be obscured and his will weakened. Madness immediately ensues. The hatred of sin, the fear of the Lord, and the sense of Christ's love and presence depart and leave the heart a prey to the enemy.

Finally, temptation gives fuel to our lusts by inciting and provoking them, so that they are embroiled in endless turmoil. One temptation—whether it is a lust, or a warped attitude, or anything else—becomes one's whole obsession. We might cite the carnal fear of Peter, the pride of Hezekiah, the covetousness of

Achan, the uncleanness of David, the worldliness of Demas, or the ambition of Diotrephes. We do not know the pride, fury, and madness of a wrong deed until we face a suitable temptation. How tragic is the life of someone whose mind is darkened, whose affections are entangled, and whose lusts are enflamed, so that his defenses break down. What hope remains for him?

We observe this power of temptation both socially and personally. Public temptations, such as those mentioned in Revelation 3:10, "try them that dwell upon the earth." They also come in a combination of persecution and seduction to test a careless generation of believers. Such public temptations take varied forms.

First, public temptations come as the result of God's judgment on those who neglect or disdain the gospel, or who, as false believers, act as traitors. God permitted Satan to seduce Ahab as a punishment (see 1 Kings 22:22). When the world yields to folly and false worship in their neglect of the truth and in the barrenness of their lives, God sends "a strong delusion, that they should believe a lie" (2 Thess. 2:11). This delusion comes with a judicial purpose to those who are selfish, spiritually slothful, careless, and worldly. As well, those who do not retain God in their hearts, God gives up to a reprobate mind (see Rom. 1:28).

Second, some public temptations spread infectiously from those who should be godly, but who are mere professors. Christ warns, "Because iniquity shall abound, the love of many shall wax cold" (Matt. 24:12). When some become negligent, careless, worldly, and wanton, they corrupt others. "A little leaven leaveneth the whole lump" (1 Cor. 5:6; Gal. 5:9). The root of bitterness that troubles a man also defiles many (see Heb. 12:15). Little by little some mere professors of the truth influence others for evil.

Third, public temptations, when accompanied by strong reasons and influence, are too hard to overcome. This often takes place gradually. When a colony of people moves from one country to another, it soon adjusts to the customs of the local inhabitants. Likewise, prosperity often makes people morally careless, and it slays the foolish and wounds the wise.

We also see the power of temptation personally. These personal temptations enter the soul by their union with lust. John speaks of "the lust of the flesh, the lust of the eyes, and the pride of life" (1 John 2:16). They reside principally in the heart and not in the world. Yet they are "in the world" because the world enters into them, mixes with them, and unites with them. By such means, temptation penetrates so deep into the heart that no antidote reaches it. It is like gangrene that mixes poison with the bloodstream.

Moreover, it is important to see that in whatever part of the soul lust resides, it affects the whole person. A lust of the mind (such as ambition, or vanity, or something similar) affects everything else. Temptation draws the whole person into it.

But some will argue: "Why be so concerned about temptation? Are we not commanded to 'count it all joy when we fall into diverse temptations'?" (James 1:2). Yes, we should accept these trials. The same apostle admonishes the wealthy to "rejoice in that he is made low" (1:10). But James adds, "Blessed is the man that endureth temptation: for when he is tried, he shall receive the crown of life" (1:12). While God may try us, He never entices us. Everyone is tempted by his own lusts. Let us make sure that our own weaknesses do not entice us and thus seduce us.

As well, the objection may be raised that our Savior Himself faced temptation. Is it evil to find ourselves in a similar state? Hebrews 2:17–18 makes it clear that it is advantageous to us that Christ was tempted. He uses, as the ground of great promise to His disciples, the fact that they had been with Him in His temptations (see Luke 22:28). Yes, it is true that our Savior experienced temptation. But Scripture reckons His temptations among the *evils* that befell Him in the days of His flesh, coming to Him through the malice of the world and its prince. He did not deliberately cast Himself into temptation. Instead He said, "Thou shalt not tempt the Lord thy God" (Matt. 4:7). Moreover, while Christ only had the *suffering* part of temptation, we also have the *sinning* part of it. He remained undefiled, but we become defiled.

Finally, some may argue, why should we be so careful about temptation when we have God's assurances? "God is faithful, who will not suffer us to be tempted above what we are able, but will with the temptation also make a way of escape" (1 Cor. 10:13). "The Lord knoweth how to deliver the godly out of temptations" (2 Peter 2:9). Yes, God has given us these assurances, but it is questionable whether God will deliver us if we willingly enter into temptation. "Shall we continue in sin, that grace may abound?" (Rom. 6:1).

It is wrong for us to enter deliberately into temptation and to think only of the near escape of our souls. We need to regard the comfort, joy, and peace of our spirits and to realize that we sojourn here for the honor of the gospel and the glory of God.

CHAPTER 10

THE DANGERS OF TEMPTATION

Having surveyed the power of temptation, we now want to consider the dangers of temptation's inception. Often we wonder if we have committed a specific sin. Rather, we should ask, "Have I entered into temptation?" We enter into temptation whenever we are drawn into sin, for all sin is from temptation (see James 1:14–15). Sin is the fruit that comes only from that root. Even to be surprised or overtaken in a fault is to be tempted. The apostle says, "Consider yourself, lest you also be tempted" (Gal. 6:1). Often we repent of the sins that overtake us, without realizing how temptation starts in the first place. This makes us vulnerable to fall once more into sin.

Entering into temptation occurs in various ways. It often begins in a concealed and subtle way. For example, a man begins by having a reputation for piety, or wisdom, or learning. People speak well of him. His vanity is tickled to hear it, and then his reputation affects his pride and ambition. If this continues, he begins to seek it actively, using all his energies to build up his own esteem, reputation, and self-glory. Having this secret eye to its expansion, he enters into temptation. If he does not deal with this quickly and ruthlessly, he will become a slave to lust.

This happens to many scholars. They find themselves esteemed and favored for their learning. This secretly appeals to their pride and ambition, and they begin to major on promoting their learning. While they do good things, it is always with an eye on the approval of others. In the end it is all carnal, making "provision for the flesh, to fulfil the lusts thereof" (Rom. 13:14).

It is true that God in His mercy sometimes overrules such false motives. In spite of the ambition, pride, and vanity of the servant, God comes in grace to turn him to Himself and to rob him of his Egyptian lusts. Then once more, God consecrates the tabernacle that once housed idols.

But it is not only learning that temptation subtly corrupts. Temptation makes every profession and vocation a potential snare. Some find themselves the darlings, the celebrities, the popular ones in their own circle of friends and associates. Once these thoughts enter into their hearts, temptation entangles them. Instead of seeking to gain more glory, they need to lie in the dust, out of a sense of the vileness in themselves.

Likewise, when a man knows that he likes preaching the gospel or some other work of the ministry, many things begin to work in his favor. His ability, his simple presentation of the message, his constant exposure before the public, and his success in it all, expose him to temptation. These things become fuel for temptation. Whatever we like to do tends to feed our lusts and tends to cause us to enter into temptation, whether it is initially good or bad.

A man enters into temptation whenever his lusts find an opportunity for temptation. As I have already stated, to enter into temptation is not merely to face temptation, but to become entangled by its power. It is almost impossible to escape from temptation if it appropriately meets one's lusts. If ambassadors come from the king of Babylon, Hezekiah's pride will cast him into temptation. If Hazael is made king of Syria, his cruelty and ambition will make him rage savagely against Israel. If the priests come with their pieces of silver, Judas' covetousness will immediately operate to sell his Master.

We see many examples of this situation in our own day. How mistaken people are who think they can play over the hole of an asp and not be stung, or touch tar without being defiled, or set their clothes on fire and not be burnt. So if something in your business, your lifestyle, or your culture suits your lusts, you have already entered into temptation. If we have a propensity for unclean thoughts, ambition in high places, sexual passion, perusal of bad literature, or anything else, temptation will use various things in our society to entrap us.

Furthermore, when someone acts weak, negligent, or casual in a duty—performing it carelessly or lifelessly, without any genuine satisfaction, joy, or interest—he has already entered into the spirit that will lead him into trouble. How many we see today who have departed from warmhearted service and have become negligent, careless, and indifferent in their prayer life or in the reading of the Scriptures. For each one who escapes this peril, a hundred others will be ensnared. Then it may be too late to acknowledge, "I neglected private prayer," or "I did not meditate on God's Word," or "I did not hear what I should have listened to." Like Sardis, we maintain dead performances and duties in our spiritual life (see Rev. 3:1).

In the Song of Solomon, the bride acknowledges, "I sleep" (Song. 5:2). Then she says, "I have put off my coat, and cannot put it on," which speaks of her reluctance to commune with her Lord (5:3). When she finally answers the door, her "beloved had withdrawn himself" (5:6). Christ had gone. Although she looks for Him, she does not find Him. This illustrates the intrinsic relationship of the new nature of the

Christian and the worship of Christ. The new nature is fed, strengthened, increased, and sweetened by Christ. Our desire focuses on God, as the psalmist describes throughout Psalm 119. Yet temptation attempts to intervene and disrupt this relationship and desire.

VIGILANCE AGAINST
THE DANGERS OF TEMPTATION

How then can we be vigilant, so that we "watch and pray"? (Matt. 26:41). This injunction from our Lord implies that we should maintain a clear, abiding apprehension of the great danger we face if we enter into temptation. If one is always aware of the great danger, one will always stand guard.

1. Always remember the great danger it is for anyone to enter into temptation.

It is sad to find most people so careless about this. Most people think about how to avoid open sin, but they never think about the dynamics of temptation within their hearts. How readily young people mix with all sorts of company. Before they realize it, they enjoy evil company. Then it is too late to warn them about the dangers of wrong companions. Unless God snatches them in a mighty way from the jaws of destruction, they will be lost.

How many plead for their "freedom," as they call it. They argue that they can do what they like and try what they want, so they run here and there to every seducer and salesman of false opinions. And what is the result? Few go unhurt, and the majority lose their faith. Let no one fear sin without also fearing temptation. They are too closely allied to be separated. Satan has put them so close together that it is very hard to separate them. He hates not the fruit, who delights in the root.

We need a moral sensitivity to the weakness and corruption within us. We need to guard against the reality and guile of Satan. We need to recognize the evil of sin and the power of temptation to work against us. If we remain careless and cold, we shall never escape its entanglements. We need to constantly remind ourselves of the danger of the entry of temptation.

2. Realize we cannot keep ourselves from falling into temptation.

But for the grace of God, we will fall into it. We have no power or wisdom to keep ourselves from entering into temptation, other than the power and wisdom of God. In all things we "are kept by the power of God" (1 Peter 1:5). "I pray," our Savior says to the Father, "not that thou shouldest take them out of the world, but that thou shouldest keep them from the evil" (John 17:15). In other words, Christ prays that the Father would guard us against the temptation of the world to enter into evil and sin.

Let our hearts admit, "I am poor and weak. Satan is too subtle, too cunning, too powerful; he watches constantly for advantages over my soul. The world presses in upon me with all sorts of pressures, pleas, and pretenses. My own corruption is violent, tumultuous, enticing, and entangling. As it conceives sin, it wars within me and against me. Occasions and opportunities for temptation are innumerable. No wonder I do not know how deeply involved I have been with sin. Therefore, on God alone will I rely for my keeping. I will continually took to Him."

If we commit ourselves to God in this way, three things will follow. First, we will experience the reality of the grace and compassion of God. He calls the fatherless and the helpless to rest upon Him. No soul has ever lacked God's supply when he depended upon God's invitation to trust in Him absolutely.

Second, we will be conscious of our danger and of our need for God's protection.

Third, we will act in faith on the promises of God to keep us. To believe that He will preserve us is, indeed, a means of preservation. God will certainly preserve us and make a way of escape for us out of the temptation, should we fall. We are to pray for what God has already promised. Our requests are to be regulated by His promises and commands. Faith embraces the promises and so finds relief. This is what James 1:5–7 teaches us. What we need, we must "ask of God." But we must "ask in faith," for otherwise we will not "receive any thing of the Lord."

God has promised to keep us in all our ways. We shall be guided in such a way that we "shall not err therein" (Isa. 35:8). He will lead us, guide us, and deliver us from the evil one. Base your life upon faith in such promises, and expect a good and assuring life. We cannot conceive of the blessings that will ensue from this attitude of trust in the promises of Christ.

3. Resist temptation by making prayer of first importance.

Praying that we enter not into temptation is a means to preserve us from it. People often talk about their wonderful experiences in maintaining this attitude of prayer, yet less than half its excellence, power, and efficacy is ever known. Whoever wishes to avoid temptation must pray. "Let us therefore come boldly unto the throne of grace, that we may obtain mercy, and find grace to help in time of need" (Heb. 4:16). By doing this, our souls are set against every form of temptation.

After Paul instructs us to "put on the whole armour of God" (that we may stand and resist in the time of temptation), he adds: "Praying always with all prayer and supplication in the Spirit, and watching thereunto, with all perseverance and supplication" (Eph. 6:11, 18). Without this attitude, we lack any real help.

Consider Paul's exhortation. "Praying always" means at all times and seasons (compare 1 Thess. 5:17). "With all prayer and supplication in the Spirit" implies expressing desires to God that are suited to our needs according to His will, by the assistance of the Holy Spirit. "Watching thereunto" means we are never distracted from this essential stance. "With all perseverance" means this is more than a passing whim, but a permanent inclination. By doing this we will stand.

If we do not abide in prayer, we will abide in temptation. Let this be one aspect of our daily intercession: "God, preserve my soul and keep my heart and all its ways so that I will not be entangled." When this is true in our lives, a passing temptation will not overcome us. We will remain free while others lie in bondage.

CHAPTER 11

WATCHING AGAINST TEMPTATION

A long with prayer, our Lord directs us to "watch" (Matt. 26:41). We especially need to watch when we are enjoying unusual prosperity, when we are neglecting the grace of God, when we are enjoying great fellowship with God, and when we are acting in self-confidence. At these times we need to watch the approaches of temptation, for it will seek to assault us.

WATCH THE TIME OF TEMPTATION

1. We face temptation in times of prosperity.

Success itself contains many different temptations. It is a time when we are lulled to forget the need of grace. In such circumstances the soul often encounters temptation and provides food and fuel for it. God's Word reminds us, "The prosperity of fools destroys them" (Prov. 1:32). It hardens them in their way, makes them despise instruction, and puts the evil day of reckoning far from them.

Without special help, prosperity is also an inconceivably malignant influence on believers. For this reason, Agur prays against riches, saying, "Lest I be full, and deny thee, and say, Who is the LORD?" (Prov. 30:9). This is so often the complaint of God against His people; when they are filled, they forget the

Lord (see Hos. 13:6). We know how David erred when he said, "In my prosperity ... I shall never be moved" (Ps. 30:6). After he boasted, he learned God had left him: "Thou didst hide thy face, and I was troubled" (30:7).

How do we respond to prosperity? We rejoice in the God of mercies. Solomon tells us, "In the day of prosperity rejoice" (Eccl. 7:14). But he also warns us to consider, lest evil lie at the door. Prosperity is an advantageous time for Satan to operate. At such times, we need a ballast to balance ourselves and give poise to our hearts. The formality of religion so easily creeps in, laying the soul open to temptation's full power.

Satisfaction and delight in creature comforts—the poison of the soul—tend to grow upon us. A hardness or lack of spiritual sense develops with success. We need to watch and fear always, but especially in times of prosperity.

2. We face temptation in times of indifference to grace, neglect of communion with God, and formality in duty.

We have mentioned the incident of the three disciples asleep in the Garden, when Jesus warned, "Arise, watch, and pray" (Matt. 26:41; Luke 22:46). We have referred to the passage in the Song of Solomon when the bride was also asleep (see 5:2–6). We have also cited the church of Sardis where the things that remained were "ready to die" (Rev. 3:2). "Be watchful," says our Savior, "and strengthen them," or worse things will come.

We need to ask, "Is my zeal cold?" Is my heart not warmed by the love of God? Are we negligent in duties of prayer or of listening to the Word? Have we become feeble in our profession of the faith? Is our delight in God's people faint? Has it grown cold? Is our love for them merely carnal? If we find ourselves in such a lethargic condition, we need to wake up!

3. We experience temptation after enjoying great fellowship with God.

The apostle Paul enjoyed glorious spiritual revelations of God and Jesus Christ. Immediately, Satan fell upon him and buffeted him so that Paul earnestly begged God to take this thorn away. Instead, he continued to struggle with it (see 2 Cor. 12).

Sometimes God gives us special discoveries of Himself and of His love and fills our hearts with His kindness. We experience unspeakable, glorious joy. One might think this is the most secure condition in the world. Like Peter, the soul cries out, "It is good for us to be here, to abide here forever" (Mark 9:5). Yet frequently some bitter temptation soon approaches us. Satan will see that we neglect many opportunities of fellowship with God in such times, so that he can then enter and take advantage of us.

Besides this, men cheat their own souls with their fanciful sense of the love of God. Then, when they discover that they have been deluded by their own emotional experiences, they become very depressed and vulnerable to all manner of temptations. Where will they find relief for their consciences, when they have been so deluded by foolish fancies of their own emotions?

Do we not see examples every day of people who are walking in the ways of the world and in their vanities, and yet who are boasting of their sense of the love of God? Should we believe them? We cannot, if we desire to know the truth. How pathetic is their true condition.

4. We face temptation in times of self-confidence.

We remember the case of Peter. We note his confidence when the poor man stood on the brink of that temptation that cost him such bitter tears. Peter boasted, "I will not deny thee. Although all should deny thee, I will not. Even if I were to die with thee, I would not deny thee" (Mark 14:29, 31).

Peter learned later to know his own heart. When he had received more of the Holy Spirit and power, he acted with much less self-confidence. He saw that it was best that others should have less confidence as well. Thus he persuades all men "to pass the time of your sojourning here in fear" (1 Peter 1:17). If they had overconfidence, he knew they would fall as he had fallen.

At his first trial, Peter compared himself with others: "Although all should forsake you, yet I will not" (Mark 14:29). But our Savior came to him and asked directly, "Simon, son of Jonas, do you love me more than these?" (John 21:15). Peter did not compare himself with others, but only cried out: "Lord, you know that I love you." No longer would he lift himself above other people. Likewise Paul says, "Be not highminded, but fear. Let him who thinks he stands take heed lest he fall" (Rom. 11:20; 1 Cor. 10:12).

Who would have thought that Peter—who had walked on the sea with Christ, who had confessed Him to be the Son of God, who had been with Him on the Mount of Transfiguration (where he heard the voice from the excellent glory)—would, at the word of a maidservant, instantly swear with vehemence that he never knew Christ? Let us take heed about overconfidence. Let us also consider the times when temptation makes its approaches to the soul and fortify our heart against them.

WATCH THE APPROACHES OF TEMPTATION

It is not enough to watch our circumstances to detect the times of temptation. We must also watch our hearts to know when temptation might approach us.

We need to know our own hearts; our natural dispositions;

and the lusts, corruptions, and spiritual weaknesses that beset us. Our Savior told the disciples, "Ye know not what manner of spirit ye are of" (Luke 9:55). They had ambition and the desire for revenge. Had they known it, they would have watched themselves. David tells us he considered his ways and kept himself from the iniquity to which he was prone (see Ps. 18:23).

It is an advantage to know oneself, because temptations often lie in one's natural disposition and personality. Someone may be gentle, easygoing, and flexible, for example, and these characteristics can become great virtue. But unless they are watched, they can also become sources for many temptations. Others are earthy, or morose, or impetuous, so that envy, malice, selfishness, peevishness, hard thoughts of others, or sulkiness lies deep within them. They scarcely take a step without falling into temptation. Still others are passionate.

To avoid temptation, we each need to understand our natural temperament. By doing this, we guard against the natural treacheries within us. If you are another Jehu, watch that you do not drive ahead furiously (see 2 Kings 9:20). If you are another Jonah, be careful that you do not sulk (see Jonah 4). Or if you are another David, watch that you are not impetuous in your decisions, which may arise with all the goodness and warmth of one's natural temperament.

Just as people have differing and distinctive personalities, so they are also affected by distinctive temptations. These relate to their nature, education, and other factors. Unless we are conscious of these propensities, relationships, and dynamic possibilities, temptation will constantly entangle us. This is why it is so important to know ourselves—our temperaments and our attitudes.

Note where sin is strong and where grace is weak within you. How many never have peace of mind because of their grumbling spirit? How many render themselves useless in the world because of their peevishness? How many deeply hurt themselves because of their gentleness and sensitivity? Become acquainted with your own heart. Though it is deep, probe it; though it is obscure, search it. Though it deceives us, giving other names to its sicknesses, do not trust it.

If people did not remain strangers to themselves, they would not maintain all their lives in the same paralyzed state. But they give flattering names to their own natural weaknesses. They try to justify, palliate, or excuse the evils of their own hearts, rather than uproot and destroy them ruthlessly. They never gain a realistic view of themselves. Ineffective lives and scandal grow like branches out of this root of self-ignorance. How few truly seek to know themselves or possess the courage to do so.

We also need to lay in provisions against the approach of temptation. You may ask, "What kind of provisions are these, and where are they to be stored?" Our Savior tells us that our heart is the treasury where we lay up and draw out either good or evil (see Matt. 12:35). We need to defend our heart against the enemy. If Satan, the prince of this world, comes and finds our heart fortified against assault, he will flee (see James 4:7).

We need to keep our hearts full of a sense of the love of God. This is the greatest preservative available to us against the power of temptation in the world. Joseph demonstrates this by crying, "How then can I do this great evil, and sin against God?" (Gen. 39:9). Temptation could not hold him, but left him alone. When the love of Christ constrains us to live for Him, then we can withstand temptation.

Fill your heart with a sense of the love of God in Christ, and apply the eternal design of His grace and shed blood to yourselves. Accept all the privileges of adoption, justification, and acceptance with God. Fill your heart with thoughts of the beauty of holiness, as designed by God and made effective by His death. Then in the ordinary course of walking with God, you will experience great peace and security from temptation.

When Christians live without this sense of the love of God, or of the privileges of His shed blood, they do not know how to avoid the entanglements of temptation. Paul tells us that the peace of God will keep or garrison our hearts (see Phil. 4:7). This implies that the heart is liable to assault, yet is secure from its enemies because of the peace of God.

What is this peace of God? It is a sense of His love and favor in Jesus Christ. Let this abide in you, and it will garrison you against all assaults. Note also that this peace of God lies in direct antithesis to all the ways and means that temptation uses to approach our souls. Contending to obtain and to keep a sense of the love of God in Christ is our barrier to all the workings and insinuations of temptation. So lay in store rich provisions of the gospel, making the soul a fortified place against any assaults that may come.

Always remain alert to temptation's initial advances, so that you may know when it is upon you. Most men do not perceive their enemy until they are wounded by him. Others, while noticing all around them those deeply involved in temptation, remain utterly insensible to their own danger. They stay fast asleep, heedless of danger, until others come and tell them that their house is on fire.

Temptation eludes our casual efforts to detect it, as we have seen. Few notice it until it is too late, and then they find themselves entangled, if not already wounded. Watch to discern the traps temptation lays before you. Understand the advantages your enemies have over you because they exercise their strength and power even before they penetrate your lusts and distill their poison into your soul.

Consider the aims and tendencies of temptation. Remember that Satan and your own lusts act in concurrence with temptation. Since lust never rises up without intending the worst of evils, recognize it as an inveterate enemy of God. Look out for its first efforts, whatever pretenses it may have.

See lust as your mortal enemy. "I hate it," says the apostle (Rom. 7:15), referring to the working of lust within him. In a sense, he is saying, "It is the worst enemy I have. Oh, that it were dead and destroyed! Oh, that I were delivered out of its power!" Realize then that at the first assault of temptation you already have the most cursed and sworn enemy at hand, setting upon you for your utter ruin. This is discussed at length in my discourse "Mortification of Sin in Believers" [Part III].

Since Satan, our other enemy, seeks to beguile us as a serpent and devour us as a lion, beware of his generous proposals for friendship. Satan does not merely tempt you to break the law. His real design lies against your own interests in the gospel. He uses your sin as a bridge to get him over onto better ground to assault you concerning your interests in Christ. Perhaps today he will say, "You can venture into that sin, because you have Christ's help in spite of it." But then tomorrow he will tell you that because you have sinned, Christ is no longer yours.

Meet temptation with faith in Christ and His redemption. Engage in no parley or argument with it if you do not want to enter into temptation. Rather say, "It is Christ that died" for such sins as these (Rom. 8:34). This is "taking the shield of faith to quench all the fiery darts of the wicked" (Eph. 6:16). Faith does this by laying hold of Christ's redemptive work and love, since He suffered for our sin.

Let your temptation be what it will, whether fear, or doubt, or depression. It is not able to stand before a faith that lifts up the standard of the cross. Some cross themselves with the sign of the cross and, by virtue of that, think they scare away the devil. To act in faith in Christ crucified, however, is to truly sign ourselves and thereby overcome the wicked one (see 1 Peter 5:9).

But suppose temptation surprises the soul and entangles it? It is too late to resist the first entrance of it. What should the soul do, now that it is carried away by temptation's power?

First, beseech God again and again that it may depart from you (see 2 Cor. 12:8). If you abide in this attitude, God will either speedily deliver you out of it or give you sufficient grace not to be utterly foiled by it. But as I have said before, do not allow your thoughts to dwell upon the things that tempt you (that only causes further entanglement), but set yourself against the temptation itself. Pray that the temptation will depart. When it is taken away, you may more calmly consider the things that tempted you.

Second, fly to Christ, knowing He will help you "in time of need" (Heb. 4:16). The apostle instructs us: "In that he has been tempted, he is able to succour them that are tempted" (Heb. 2:18). In other words, when you are tempted and ready to faint, and when you want help—desperately so, or you will die—trust Christ, knowing that He also was tempted. To consider that He suffered temptation and conquered it for our sake gives us new strength. Always expect relief from Him (see Heb. 4:15–16). Lie down at His feet and make your complaint known to Him, begging for His help. You will not ask in vain.

Third, look to Him for promised deliverance. Consider that He is faithful; He will not allow you to be tempted above what you are able (see 1 Cor. 10:13). Understand that He promises to comfort us in all our trials and temptations (see 2 Cor. 1:4). Call to mind all His promises of assistance and deliverance. Ponder them in your heart. Rest upon them, knowing that God has innumerable ways to deliver you.

God may deliver you, first of all, by sending you an affliction to mortify your heart toward that temptation. While before it was a sweet morsel to the tongue, now you have no further taste or relish for it. Your desire for it has been killed.

Second, God may by some providence alter the source of your temptation. When He takes the fuel from the fire, it goes out.

Third, He may tread down Satan under your feet if he should ever dare to suggest anything that is to your disadvantage. When the God of peace does this, you will not hear from Satan anymore.

Fourth, He may give you such a supply of grace that you will be free, not perhaps from the temptation itself, but from the tendency and the danger of it. This was the experience of Paul (see 2 Cor. 12:7–10).

Fifth, He may also give you such an assurance of success in the issue that He leaves you refreshed in the midst of your trials. You are kept from the trouble of the temptation, as was the case with Paul.

Sixth, God may utterly remove the temptation and make you a complete conqueror. In these, and in innumerable other ways, God keeps you from temptation. Remember whenever temptation surprises you and makes an entry into your soul, that you have all the resources, with all speed, to repair the breach. Close up that passage into which the waters have begun to flood. Deal with your soul like a wise physician. Inquire when, how, and by what means you fell into this sickness. If you find that negligence or carelessness in keeping watch over yourself is at the bottom of it all, then focus upon this tendency or weakness. Lament before the Lord; then proceed to the work that lies before you.

CHAPTER 12

KEEPING CHRIST'S WORD AGAINST TEMPTATION

The directions that we have outlined in the previous chapters stem partly from the nature of temptation itself and partly from the nature of the circumstances in which we face temptation. But there remains for our consideration one final instruction that contains an approved antidote against the poison of temptation.

It is a remedy that Christ Himself notes has efficacy and success. It is given in the words of our Lord to the church of Philadelphia: "Because thou hast kept the word of my patience, I will also keep thee from the hour of temptation, which shall come upon all the world, to try them that dwell upon the earth" (Rev. 3:10). Christ is "the same yesterday, and to day, and for ever" (Heb. 13:8). Just as He has dealt with the church of Philadelphia, so He deals with us. If we keep the word of His patience, He will keep us from the hour of temptation. When we commit our concerns to Him, He is able to bear them. Let us consider this in more detail.

THE WORD OF CHRIST'S PATIENCE

The word of Christ is the word of the gospel. It is the word revealed to Him from the bosom of the Father. It is the word of the Word. It is the word, spoken in time, concerning the eternal Word. Scripture speaks of it as "the word of Christ" (Col. 3:16), "the gospel of Christ" (Rom. 1:16; 1 Cor. 9:12), and "the doctrine of Christ" (Heb. 6:1). It is "of Christ," which is to say, that He is its author (see Heb. 1:2). He is also the chief subject of it (see 2 Cor. 1:20). Now in Revelation 3:10 this word is called the "word of Christ's patience," which emphasizes His forbearance and tolerance. He exercises this patience especially toward all who trust Him.

First, *Christ is patient toward His saints.* He bears with them, and He suffers for them. "The Lord is ... longsuffering to usward" (2 Peter 3:9). The gospel is the word of Christ's patience to believers. He bears with so many unkindnesses, so many causeless breaches and neglects of His love, so many affronts against His grace, that His patience manifests the gospel, not only by the word of His grace, but also by the word of His patience. He suffers in all the reproaches they bring upon His name and ways. He suffers in them, for "in all their affliction he is afflicted" (Isa. 63:9).

Second, *Christ is also patient toward His elect who are not yet effectually called.* In Revelation 3:20, He stands waiting at the door of their hearts and knocks for an entrance. He deals with them by all means and yet stands and waits until "[His] head is filled with dew, and [His] locks with the drops of the night" (Song. 5:2). He endures the cold and inconveniences of the night so that when the morning comes, He may have entrance. Sometimes for a long season—while He is scorned in His person, persecuted in His saints, and reviled in His word—He stands at the door in the word of His patience, with His heart full of love toward rebellious souls.

Third, *Christ is patient to the perishing world.* The time of His kingdom in this world is called the time of His "patience" (Rev.

1:9). He "endures the vessels of wrath with much longsuffering" (Rom. 9:22). While believers share the gospel throughout the world, Christ exercises patience toward all men. This so astonishes the saints in heaven and on earth that they cry out, "How long?" (Ps. 13:1–2; Rev. 6:10). Some even consider Him as impotent as an idol (see 2 Peter 3:4). He endures from them bitter things in His name, in His ways, in His worship, in His saints, in all His interests of honor and love, yet He does not pass them by and leave them alone. He will not cut short His patience until believers proclaim the gospel no more. Patience must accompany the gospel.

KEEPING THE WORD OF CHRIST'S PATIENCE

Now it is this word of His patience that we must keep in order to escape "the hour of temptation." Three things merit our consideration concerning keeping this word: knowing it, valuing it, and obeying it.

First, anyone who desires to keep this word must know it. It is a word of grace and mercy to save him, a word of holiness and purity to sanctify him, a word of liberty and power to ennoble him and to set him free, and a word of consolation to support him in every condition.

As a word of *grace and mercy,* the word of Christ's patience saves us. "It is the power of God unto salvation" (Rom. 1:16). It is "the grace of God that bringeth salvation" (Titus 2:11). It is "the word of grace, which is able to build us up, and to give us an inheritance among all them that are sanctified" (Acts 20:32). It is "the word which is able to save our souls" (James 1:21). When the word of the gospel is known as a word of mercy, grace, and pardon; as the sole evidence for life; and as the conveyance of an eternal inheritance, then we truly live. Then we strive to keep it.

As a word of *holiness and purity,* it sanctifies us. "You are clean through the word which I have spoken unto you," says our Savior (John 15:3). We need to know that it is the word of Christ's patience that sanctifies and cleanses us (see John 17:17). The empty professors of our times remain ignorant of this truth. That is why the power of temptation so readily overwhelms many. Men full of self; full of the world; full of fury, ambition, and unclean lusts only talk unceasingly about keeping the word of Christ (see 1 Peter 1:2; 2 Tim. 2:19).

As a word of *liberty and power,* it ennobles us and sets us free from the guilt of sin and wrath. As a word of holiness, it delivers us from the power of sin. But it also keeps us from the entanglements of other men and the world. It declares us to be Christ's freemen and therefore in bondage to none (see John 8:32; 1 Cor. 7:23). This is not a freedom from proper subjection to superiors or from all duty; it is a word of freedom that gives us largeness of mind, power, and deliverance from bondage (see 1 Peter 2:16).

It is freedom of conscience in our worship of God (see Gal. 5:1). It is freedom from ignoble and slavish respect for men or for things of the world in the course of our pilgrimage. The gospel gives us a free and large and noble spirit in our subjection to God, and nothing less. This freedom operates in a spirit, "not of fear, but of power, and of love, and of a sound mind" (2 Tim. 1:7). It is a mind that is "in nothing terrified" (Phil. 1:28). It is not swayed by any undue respect for others. Nothing is more unworthy of the gospel than a mind in bondage to persons or to things, prostituting itself to the lusts of men and to the fears of the world. He who truly knows the word of Christ's patience is free from innumerable and unspeakable temptations.

As a word of *consolation,* it supports us in every circumstance so that we lack nothing. It is a word we attend to with "joy unspeakable and full of glory" (see 1 Peter 1:8). It gives support, relief, refreshment, satisfaction, peace, consolation, joy, and glory in whatever condition one finds himself To know the word of Christ's patience is to know the gospel. To a significant degree this is a condition for our preservation from the hour and power of temptation.

Second, we must value the word of Christ's patience, keeping it a treasure (see 2 Tim. 1:14). Because it is a good treasure and a faithful word, the apostle says, hold it fast (see Titus 1:9). It is a word that comprises the whole interest of Christ in the world. Value it as your chief treasure. This is what it means to keep the word of Christ's patience. Anyone who seeks the help of Christ in the time of temptation will not neglect His Word.

Third, we must obey the word of Christ's patience. John 14:15 reminds us that we cannot keep Christ's word without obeying His commandments. Close adherence to Christ in all things, especially in the midst of the world's opposition to the gospel of Christ, demonstrates our obedience to the word of His patience. This intent of the mind and spirit requires the care of the heart and the diligence of the whole person in keeping this word.

If we have an intimate acquaintance with the gospel in all its excellence, knowing the word as one of mercy, holiness, freedom, and consolation, we will value it as our chief and only treasure. We will also make it our business to give ourselves to it in absolute obedience. Then when there is opposition and apostasy that tests the patience of Christ to the utmost, God will preserve us from the hour of temptation.

How God Keeps Us in the Hour of Temptation

Do not let anyone think that he can avoid temptation without giving serious consideration to all that has been said. We must

never separate God's promise to keep us in the hour of temptation from our responsibility to keep the word of Christ's
patience.

1. Christ's word of patience includes God's pledge to keep us.

Christ solemnly gave this promise to the church at Philadelphia.
In Revelation 3:10 He promises to keep those who keep His word
from the great trial and temptation that was to come upon all the
world. The fulfillment of this promise involves all three Persons
of the Trinity.

The faithfulness of the Father accompanies the promise. We
shall be kept in temptation because "God is faithful, who will
not suffer you to be tempted" (1 Cor. 10:13). "He is faithful
who promised" (Heb. 10:23). "He will remain faithful; he cannot deny himself" (2 Tim. 2:13). When we stand under this
promise, the faithfulness of God works on our behalf for our
protection.

Every promise of God also contains the covenant grace of the
Son. He promises, "I will keep you" (Rev. 3:10). How? "By my
grace that is with you" (see 1 Cor. 15:10). Paul suffered intensely
from temptation. He "besought the Lord" for help, and God
answered, "My grace is sufficient for you" (2 Cor. 12:9). Paul could
add, "I will glory in my infirmities, that the power of Christ may
rest upon me." The efficacy of the grace of Christ becomes evident
in our preservation (see Heb. 2:18; 4:16).

The efficacy of the Holy Spirit accompanies God's promises,
as well. He is called "the Holy Spirit of promise" (Eph. 1:13).
This is not only because He promised the advent of Christ, but
because He effectively makes good the promise within us. He
preserves the soul of the one who follows these promises (see
Isa. 59:21).

2. God preserves us as we keep the word of Christ's patience.

When we keep Christ's word, we guard our heart against temptable tendencies. David prayed, "Let integrity and uprightness preserve me" (Ps. 25:21). God gave him a disposition that left no entry points for temptation to penetrate. In contrast, we read: "There is no peace for the wicked" (Isa. 57:21). The wicked face temptation as a troubled sea, full of restlessness and storms. They have no peace. God delivers us from such troubles as we guard our hearts to keep Christ's word.

Negatively, we guard our hearts by mortification. The apostle James indicates that temptations arise from our own lusts (James 1:14). By eliminating them, we destroy the entry points for temptation. Paul says, "I am crucified with Christ" (Gal. 2:20). To keep close to Christ is to be crucified with Him and to be dead to all the carnal desires of the world. Achan failed to mortify the lusts of his heart. When he saw "a goodly Babylonish garment, and two hundred shekels of silver, and a wedge of gold," he "coveted them" first; then he "took them" (Josh. 7:21). Sin seduced him. But a mortified heart and a crucified life will preserve us from these things.

Positively, we guard our hearts by filling them with better concerns and values. The apostle Paul reckoned the things of the world mere loss and dung (see Phil. 3:8). The new is so much better. As we daily taste the gracious goodness of the Lord, all else becomes worthless in comparison. One fills his heart with these better things by maintaining three concerns.

His first concern is *Christ Himself.* The love and presence of Christ always stay with him. He knows Christ is concerned about his honor and that His plan is to "present him holy, and unblameable, and unreproveable in his sight" (Col. 1:22). His Spirit is grieved when this work is interrupted (see Eph. 4:30).

Because he knows Christ's intention, he avoids resisting His purposes, expressing contempt for His honor, despising His love, or trampling His gospel into the mud. Dwelling in his heart is the constraining love of Christ (see 2 Cor. 5:14).

His second concern is *Christ's own victories over temptations.* Christ's life on earth included His triumphs over the frequent assaults of the Evil One. He resisted all, He conquered all, and He has become the Captain of salvation to those who obey Him (see Heb. 2:10). How can any follower of Christ deny the reality of His victory by living as a defeated Christian because of temptation in his life?

His third concern is *approval.* He has learned to enjoy the favor of Christ, to sense His love, to appreciate His acceptance, and to converse with Him. He cannot bear to become separated from Christ, as the spouse declared in Song of Solomon 3:4. Once she recognized Him, in no way would she let Him out of her sight. Never again would she lose His presence.

When a believer keeps the word of Christ's patience, it does not merely influence his concerns. It also affects the governing principles of his life.

First, he lives by faith in God (see Gal. 2:20). Faith works in all areas of his heart, emptying his soul of its own wisdom, understanding, and self-sufficiency, so that it may act now in the wisdom and fullness of Christ. Proverbs 3:5 gives us sound advice to guard against temptation: "Trust in the LORD with all thine heart; and lean not upon thine own understanding." This is the work of faith: to trust God and to live in such trust of Him. When a man trusts himself, "his own counsel shall cast him down" (Job 18:7). Only faith empties us of our own self-sufficiency. We should not live to ourselves and by ourselves, but only for Christ, by Christ, and in Christ.

Second, he lives with concern for others. He shows love for

God's people by not causing them to stumble over his temptations. David prays in Psalm 69:6, "Let not them that wait on thee, O Lord GOD of hosts, be ashamed for my sake: let not those that seek thee be confounded for my sake, O God of Israel." In other words, "Do not let me so misbehave that others, for whom I would lay down my life, should be ill spoken of, dishonored, reviled, and condemned because of my own failings." When someone preoccupies himself with the well-being of others, God saves him. In contrast, a self-centered man falls.

If God has promised that He will keep us, why do so many professors of Christianity fall into temptation? Is it not simply because they do not keep the word of Christ's patience? Because of disobedience, Paul says, "many are weak and sickly among you, and many sleep" (1 Cor. 11:30). God chastens all those who fail to keep Christ's Word and neglect to walk closely with Him.

It would take too long to cite all the ways professors of Christianity fail to keep Christ's Word. We can simply summarize four ways they often fail. First, they conform to the world when Christ would redeem us from its delights and promiscuous compliances. Second, they neglect the duties that Christ has enjoined upon us to fulfill, from personal meditation on the one hand to public duties on the other. Third, they strive and disagree among themselves, despising each other and acting indifferent to the bond of communion between saints. Fourth, they make selfishness the end of life. When these traits characterize people, then the word of Christ's patience is fruitless among them, and God will not keep them from temptation.

FINAL EXHORTATIONS

If we want God to preserve us in the hour of temptation, we will take heed against anything that would distract us from keeping the word of Christ's patience. The following cautions will help us.

First, do not trust your own advice, understanding, and reasoning. Second, even if you discipline yourself earnestly (by prayer, fasting, and other such measures) to safeguard against a particular lust, you will still fail if you neglect such other matters as worldliness, compliance, looseness of living, or moral negligence. Third, while it is God's purpose to give the saints security, perseverance, and preservation from general apostasy, yet we must never use this as an excuse to abuse some other aspect of our walk with God. Many relieve their consciences with "cheap grace," only to find their perplexities intensified in other areas of life.

In addition, seek to determine the relevance of God's Word to the particular context of your temptations. First, when you encounter the cult of celebrities, observe from His Word how God overturns the values of human popularity. Second, consider the ways God sees things differently from the world. If you do so, you will be content to remain unnoticed by the world. Third, notice how God emphasizes faith and prayer. Esteem them better than all the strength and councils of men. Fourth, seek to recover God's ordinances and institutions from the carnal administrations that are under the bondage of men's lusts. Bring them forth in the beauty and power of the Holy Spirit.

The nature of worldliness is to neglect the word of Christ's patience. It slights God's people and judges them by the standards of the world. It relies on human counsel and understanding. It allows unsanctified people to walk in God's temple and to trample His ordinances. In all these ways let us remain watchful. Let us keep the word of Christ's patience if we cherish our safety. In this frame of mind, plead with the Lord Jesus Christ, in the light of His promises, to help you in your need. Approach Him as your merciful High Priest.

If you visited a hospital and asked how each patient fell ill, no doubt each would reply, "It was by this or that circumstance that I contracted the disease." After hearing them, would it not make you much more careful not to fall into their circumstances?

Or if you went to a prison, you might ask different criminals how they received their sentence. Would you not be warned that sin leads to certain judgment? "Can a man take fire into his bosom, and his clothes not be burnt? Can one go upon hot coals, and his feet not be burned?" (Prov. 6:27–28). Do we only realize the invincible power of temptation once it captures us? We conclude with three warnings.

First, if you ignore temptation, even though our Savior commands us to be vigilant as the only safeguard against it, then remember Peter. Perhaps you have been fortunate so far to escape trouble in spite of your carelessness. But wake up, and thank God for His gentleness and patience with you.

Second, remember that you are always under the scrutiny of Christ, the great Captain of our salvation (see Heb. 2:10). He has enjoined us to watch and pray that we enter not into temptation (see Matt. 26:41). As He saw the gathering storm, He alerted His disciples with this warning. Does not His reproof grieve you? Or are you unafraid to hear His thunder against you for your neglect? (see Rev. 3:2).

Third, realize that if you neglect this duty and then fall into temptation—which assuredly you will do—God may also bring heavy affliction upon you. He may even bring judgment, as evidence of His anger. You will not consider this warning mere empty words when it actually happens to you. Then what woe will betide you if you are not found full of godly sorrow.

Let us keep our spirits unentangled by avoiding all appearance of evil and all the ways that lead there. Guard yourself especially in your social contacts and your occupations, which all contain pitfalls to entrap us.

PART III

MORTIFICATION OF SIN
IN BELIEVERS

*If ye through the Spirit do mortify
the deeds of the body, ye shall live.*
Romans 8:13

CHAPTER 13

THE CHARACTER OF MORTIFICATION

Iconsented to publish this discourse for two reasons. First, as I have considered the present state of professing Christians, I have seen a great lack of ability among many to deal with temptations. While they may have peace in the world, they suffer from tensions and divisions among themselves.

Second, I have seen the dangerous mistakes of some who give direction in spiritual discipline. Because they remain unacquainted with the mystery of the gospel and the efficacy of the death of Christ, they impose unnecessary yokes upon their disciples. Their view of mortification is unrelated to the nature of the gospel and not subject to its means and effects. This results in superstition, self-righteousness, and anxiety of conscience in those who submit to these false forms of discipline.

What I propose to humbly express here in the spirit and truth of the gospel is a biblical view of mortification—emphasizing the reality of the covenant of grace. Having preached on this subject with some gracious assurance, I have been urged by various people to publish this material. Certainly, it is the chief desire of my life to promote discipline and holiness in my own heart, as well as in others, to the glory of God. May this treatise adorn the gospel of our Lord Jesus Christ in all things.

MORTFICATION IS ESSENTIAL FOR BELIEVERS

We find the foundation of Christian discipline expressed by the apostle in Romans 8:13: "If ye live after the flesh, ye shall die: but if ye through the Spirit do mortify the deeds of the body, ye shall live."

Five points should be noted about the last half of this verse:

- A *condition* is stated: "if."
- A *subject* is denoted: "ye" (believers).
- A *means* is identified: "through the Spirit."
- A *duty* is prescribed: "mortify the deeds of the body."
- A *promise* is given: "ye shall live."

It is the first point, the *conditional* "if," that stands out as crucial. Conditionals in such propositions denote two things. First, they imply the uncertainty of the events promised, for the condition is absolutely necessary for what follows. Second, they suggest the certainty of the coherence and connection between the things mentioned. Doctors promise a sick patient, "If you take this prescription, you will regain your health." They imply the certainty of the connection between the remedy and health when they make such a conditional statement.

This connection in Romans 8:13, however, is not between cause and effect. Instead, it is the connection between means and end. God has appointed the means of mortification through the Spirit to achieve the end, life. If you use this means, you will live.

Next, note the *subject* to whom this duty is prescribed. "Ye" (believers) are the subject of this mortification. It is characteristic of much Pharisaism to press this duty immediately upon others in self-righteousness. But it is we believers who need to accept this duty. Even the choicest saints who seek to remain free from the condemning power of sin need to make it their business, as long as they live, to mortify the indwelling power of sin.

Third, note that the Holy Spirit is the principal *means* to accomplish this duty. The Spirit mentioned here is identified as "the Spirit of God" in verses 9 and 14, "the Spirit of Christ" in verses 9 and 11, "the Spirit of adoption" in verse 15, and "the Spirit that maketh intercession for the saints" in verse 26.

All other ways of discipline are in vain. All other helps leave us helpless. Mortification is only accomplished "through the Spirit." As Paul intimates in Romans 9:30–32, many attempt to do this based on other principles and in other ways. But this is the work of the Spirit; by Him alone is it wrought. No other power can accomplish it. Mortification based on human strength, carried out with man-made schemes, always ends in self-righteousness. This is the essence and substance of all false religion in the world.

Fourth, note that the *duty* of discipline is to "mortify the deeds of the body." This raises three questions for our consideration: What is meant by the term "body"? What are the "deeds" of the body? And what is meant by the term "mortify"?

The *body* at the close of the verse is the same as the "flesh" at the beginning of the verse—"If ye live after the flesh, ye shall die." The apostle draws an antithesis between this "flesh" and the "Spirit." Thus the body is all the corruption and depravity of our natures, which the body literally shares in large part. It is indwelling sin, the corrupted flesh or lust, that is intended here. Paul speaks of it in Romans 6:6 as "the old man," or "the body of sin." It is the embodiment of warped affections and the seat of all lusts.

The *deeds* of the body are described in Galatians 5:19 as "the works of the flesh." The apostle says they are "manifest" and then enumerates seventeen specific deeds. "The passions and lusts of the flesh" (Gal. 5:24) produce fruit and deeds. It is in this sense that Paul speaks of the body as "dead because of sin" (Rom. 8:10). That is their result.

To *mortify* is literally to put to death. "If you put to death," argues the apostle, "you kill." Indwelling sin in the believer is the old man who must be killed, with all his faculties, properties, wisdom, craft, subtlety, and strength. Its power, life, vigor, and strength must be destroyed and slain by the cross of Christ. The old man must be "crucified with Christ" (Rom. 6:6), if we would experience regeneration (see Rom. 6:3–5). But this whole work is gradual and requires all the days of our life for its accomplishment. God has designed this mortification of the indwelling sin that remains in our mortal bodies in order to eliminate the life and power of our flesh.

Finally, note the *promise* given in this duty—"ye shall live." God promises us life, in contrast to the threat of death by the flesh. "The flesh reaps corruption" (Gal. 6:8), which is destruction from God.

This promise of life, however, is not the essence of life (we already have that spiritual life in Christ, as believers). It is the joy, comfort, and vigor of the life in Christ, which we can always experience to a greater degree. Paul says to the Thessalonians, "Now I live, if you stand fast" (1 Thess. 3:8). In other words, "If you live this way, you will lead a good, vigorous, comfortable, spiritual life while you live on earth, and I will be comforted and rejoice in my life as well." Thus the vigor, power, and comfort of our spiritual lives depend upon the mortification of the deeds of the flesh.

A BIBLICAL DEFINITION OF MORTFICATION

It is important that we understand the work of mortification before we consider our need to practice this duty. Let us examine the true meaning of mortification by first refuting several false notions about it.

The first thing to remember is that the mortification of sin never means the death and final elimination of sin. This cannot be expected in this life. Paul admits, "Not as though I had already attained, either were already perfect" (Phil. 3:12). He was a choice saint, whose example others could follow (see 3:17). But he still had a vile body and looked for the final change that only Christ would accomplish (see 3:21). God sees that it is best for us never to be complete in ourselves, but only to be "complete in Christ" (Col. 2:10).

Second, mortification does not consist of pretending sin is removed. That would only add hypocrisy to iniquity. One would have another heart perhaps, but it would only be more cunning, not more holy.

In addition, mortification does not mean the improvement of a quiet, controlled temperament. Some people are naturally reserved. Yet it is easy to believe that if we develop our self-control, prudence, and other qualities, we have really changed. But our hearts may still stink like a cesspool of corruption. On the other hand, someone may be plagued all his life with a bad temper. Yet in his struggles he may know more of mortification than the naturally reserved person. Mortification is not achieved by refining those temperaments that come naturally to us.

Moreover, a sin is not mortified when it is only diverted. Simon Magus left all his sorcery for a time. But his covetousness and ambitions remained. Peter tells him, "I perceive you are in the gall of bitterness" (Acts 8:23). In spite of all his efforts to reform, he was still the same old Simon Magus. To barter lusts, to exchange one for another, is no remedy. To change pride for worldliness, sensuality for Pharisaism, or vanity for contempt is not mortification of sin.

Furthermore, occasional conquests of sin do not count as mortification. When a person faces some sudden invasion of sin in his life—such as a scandal or some evil tragedy—and becomes all stirred up about it, he may feel he has mortified sin. He reacts to sin as fervently as the Corinthians did in 2 Corinthians 7:11. But when the lust dies down for a time, he forgets about it. Yet the lust is like a thief that has only lain low in order to start its felony once more.

Likewise, when a sinner faces the affliction of some calamity, or the exposure of some sin, he deals with the problem by resolving never to do it again. It appears that the sin is gone, whereas it is only concealed, waiting to come back later on.

Psalm 78:32–37 declares: "For all this they sinned still, and believed not for his wondrous works.... When he slew them, then they sought him.... They remembered that God was their rock, and the high God their redeemer. Nevertheless they did flatter him with their mouths, and they lied unto him with their tongues. For their heart was not right with him, neither were they stedfast in his covenant."

What then is mortification? What does it mean to mortify sin? It consists of three things.

1. Mortification is the habitual weakening of sin.

Every lust is a depraved habit or disposition that continually inclines the heart toward evil. Unmortified, it is what is described in Genesis 6:5:"Every imagination of the thoughts of [man's] heart was only evil continually." The only reason why an unregenerate man is not under the perpetual pursuit of some lust is because he is distracted by so many more of them. But the general bent is well recognized, for it is the disposition toward self-pleasing. Men are said to have their hearts set upon evil to make "provisions for the flesh" (Rom. 13:14).

Now the primary task of mortification is to weaken this habit of sin so that its power to express itself—in violence, frequency, tumult, provocation, and unrest—is quelled. Lust sometimes gains strength when it meets with a temperament that best suits it or when Satan manipulates it (as he does in a thousand ways). But lust particularly gains strength by temptation. When the two meet, sin receives new vigor, violence, and power.

Some lusts are particularly violent. Above other sins, Paul says, "Flee fornication. Every sin that a man doeth is without the body; but he that commiteth fornication sinneth against his own body" (1 Cor. 6:18). When some people avoid this more public and more tempestuous sin, their peers consider them disciplined and self-controlled. On the contrary, they simply indulge in lusts that are less conspicuous and associated with a quieter spirit. But they are still lustful.

The first expression of mortification is to weaken these lusts. Paul speaks of crucifying the "world" and the "flesh with the affections and lusts" (Gal. 5:24; 6:14). It is literally like a man who is nailed to a cross. First, he struggles and cries out with his strength, but as his blood and spirit waste away, he weakens. "Our old man," says Paul, "is crucified with Christ, that the body of sin might be destroyed" (Rom. 6:6). Why? "That henceforth we should not serve sin" or allow it to incline our hearts in sin's direction.

2. Mortification is a constant fight and contention against sin.

This is necessary when sin is strong and vigorous, and the soul scarcely makes any progress against it. David complained, "Mine iniquities have taken hold upon me, so that I am not able to look up" (Ps. 40:12). How could he fight against sin? How can we fight against it? Let us consider three things to do.

First, it is necessary to recognize the enemy you face. Take sin seriously—most seriously indeed. When people view sin superficially, they have no sense of need or motivation to mortify sin. But when a man "knows the plague of his own heart" (1 Kings 8:38), he will fear it and do something about it. When someone remains ignorant of his enemy, he justifies himself and behaves impatiently toward those who admonish or reprove him (see 2 Chron. 16:7–10).

Second, it is important to learn the wiles and tactics of sin before engaging in spiritual warfare. This is what men do in dealing with their enemies. They gather intelligence about the designs and strategies of the enemy. Without such spying and intelligence work, war would be reduced to a brutish affair. It is the same with sin. Observe the ways of evil, and then prevent them. David learned, "My sin is ever before me" (Ps. 51:3). It is important to learn the subtleties, policies, and depth of indwelling sin. Learn to recognize its typical excuses, pleas, and pretenses. Then in anticipation of its wiles, stay on guard.

Third, severely attack it, loading against sin all the firepower most destructive to its survival. Give it new wounds every day. The apostle urges, "Mortify therefore your members which are upon the earth" (Col. 3:5). Never think of sin or lust as dead because it lies dormant.

3. Mortification is evidenced by frequent success against sin.

By success, I do not mean the frustration of sin, but the pursuit of it for a complete conquest. When sin no longer hinders our duty or interrupts our peace of mind, then mortification has succeeded to some extent.

What is mortification then? First, it is the weakening of sin's indwelling disposition. Pride is weakened by the implanting and growth of humility, passion is neutralized by patience, uncleanness is washed away by purity of mind and conscience, and love of this world is checked by heavenly-mindedness. These graces come from the Holy Spirit. Second, it is the alacrity, vigor, and cheerfulness of the Spirit or new man contending against lust. Mortification succeeds in varying degrees and may completely triumph if the sin in question is not lodged too deeply within the natural temperament.

CHAPTER 14

THE NEED FOR MORTIFICATION

The *promise* of life and vigor in our spiritual life depends much upon our mortification of sin. To gain spiritual strength, we must weaken sin, disentangle our hearts from false ambitions, and cleanse our thoughts. We must also mortify our affections so that we become more engaged in the worship of God than in the worship of our own idols. Mortification prunes indwelling sin and allows the graces of God to grow with vigor in our life.

God has given us His peace and consolation (see Isa. 57:18–19). Indeed, He has given us all the privileges of adoption into His family (see Rom. 8:16). But in the ordinary course of daily life, this standing is actualized in the deeds of mortification. Mortification robs sin of its debilitating, inharmonious, and emotionally distracting influences. Without mortification, sin darkens the mind, while the lusts of the flesh grow like weeds. Mortification is the soul's vigorous opposition to the fruitless self-life.

Suppose a true Christian finds a besetting sin within himself that captivates him. It consumes his heart with trouble; it perplexes his mind; it weakens his communion with God; it upsets his peace of mind and perhaps defiles his conscience. It even begins to harden his heart because of the deceitfulness of sin. What should he do? How can he struggle to have the power to maintain strength, peace, and communion with God? He will only regain this promise of life in Christ if he mortifies the besetting sin that troubles him.

THE DAILY MORTFICATION OF SIN

The most saintly believers, who appear free from the condemning power of sin, make it their *duty* every day to mortify the indwelling power of sin. Paul exhorts us in Colossians 3:5, "Mortify therefore your members which are upon the earth." He is saying, "Make it your daily occupation. Do not cease a day from this work. Be killing sin or it will kill you." Jesus tells us the Father constantly prunes every living branch of the vine, so that it will bear more fruit (see John 15:2).

Since indwelling sin always abides in the believer, we always need to mortify it. We dare not speak "as though we had already attained, either were already perfect" (Phil. 3:12). We are to renew our inward man "day by day" (2 Cor. 4:16). Sin does not only abide with us, but it continually labors to bring forth the deeds of the flesh. Paul tells us that the law in his members is still rebelling against the law of his mind (see Rom. 7:23). Another apostle observes, "The spirit that dwells in us lusts to envy" (James 4:5). Sin is always acting, always conceiving, always seducing and tempting. To dare to stand still is to lose the battle.

Indeed, to leave sin alone is to let it bring forth great, cursed, scandalous, soul-destroying sins. In Galatians 5:19–21 the apostle describes these as "the works of the flesh." Unless we mortify sin daily and constantly, it will get the better of us and destroy us as believers. To neglect this duty is to reject the help God has given to us against our greatest enemy. To neglect this help from God is to allow the heart to become hardened by sin (see Heb.

3:13) and to weaken the whole Christian life (see Ps. 31:10; 38:5, 8; 40:12; 51:8).

It is also our duty to "grow in grace" (2 Peter 3:18), to be "perfecting holiness in the fear of God" (2 Cor. 7:1) by "renewing the inward man day by day" (2 Cor. 4:16). We cannot do this without daily mortifying sin. Sin sets its strength against every act of holiness and against every step of faith. Thus in spite of the mortification exhibited in the cross of Christ for each and every sin, we must apply its efficacy by our daily mortification of the flesh.

Every professor of faith who fails to mortify sin daily exhibits two evil characteristics. First, he has little regard for the reality of sin in his own life. The cause of this indifference is his ability to absorb and digest sins daily, without bitterness or repentance. He does not deny all ungodliness (see Titus 2:12). He is not cleansed by the blood of Christ (see 1 John 1:7; Titus 2:14). He does not escape the pollutions that are in the world through the knowledge of our Lord Jesus Christ (see 2 Peter 2:20).

Second, he deceives others in his unmortified state. He appears all right in comparison to others. He seems to walk separated from the world, yet he still lives in its ways. He talks spiritually, but he lives in vanity. He mentions his communion with God, but he is in every way conformed to the world. He boasts of the forgiveness of God, but he never forgives others. He actually deceives himself into thinking he is a partaker of eternal life.

THE SPIRIT'S POWER FOR MORTFICATION

The Holy Spirit is the only sufficient means for the work of mortification. All other ways are futile without Him. In vain do men seek other remedies. Vows, fastings, and other efforts of spiritual discipline mean little if the Holy Spirit is not present.

God never appointed these ways and means insisted upon in natural, self-imposed mortification. God asks, "Who has required these things at your hand?" (Isa. 1:12).

Jesus exposed this hypocrisy by saying, "In vain do you worship me, teaching for doctrines the traditions of men" (Matt. 15:9). The apostle concludes, "They are always learning, but never coming to a knowledge of the truth" (2 Tim. 3:7). Spiritually sick men cannot sweat out their fever by working. Duties are excellent food for the healthy soul, but they are no medicine for a sick soul.

Rather, true mortification is the work of the Holy Spirit as we trust Christ. God promised to give us the Spirit for this need. Both Ezekiel 11:19 and 36:26 promise, "I will give you my Spirit and take away your stony heart." We also experience this mortification as the gift of Christ, for without Him we can do nothing (see John 15:5).

How then does the Spirit mortify sin? First, the Holy Spirit causes our hearts to abound in grace and His fruits, which oppose the deeds of the flesh (contrast Gal. 5:19–21 and 5:22–23). Believers crucify the flesh by walking in the Spirit (see Gal. 5:16). This "renewal of us by the Holy Spirit" (Titus 3:5) is one great way of mortification. He causes us to grow, to thrive, and to abound in those graces that oppose the destructive fruits of the flesh.

Second, the Holy Spirit mortifies sin "by the spirit of judgment and the spirit of burning" (Isa. 4:4). He is the fire which burns up the very root of lust.

Third, the Holy Spirit brings the cross of Christ into our hearts by faith. He causes us to know "the fellowship of his sufferings, being made conformable unto his death" (Phil. 3:10).

Some may argue, however, "If this work can only be done by the Holy Spirit, why are we exhorted to do something about it ourselves?" First, we are commanded to mortify the deeds of the body because He works "in [us] both to will and to do of his good pleasure" (Phil. 2:13). He works "all our works in us" (Isa. 26:12). He works "the work of faith with power" (2 Thess. 1:11). He causes us to pray and is called the Spirit of supplication (see Rom. 8:26; Zech. 12:10).

Second, mortification must remain a work of our obedience to His Spirit. It is a work that preserves our free will, so we must do so with our understanding, will, affection, and conscience. He works in us and with us—not against us, or in spite of us, or without us. His assistance is an encouragement to our desires.

MORTFICATION IS FOR TRUE BELIEVERS

We cannot proceed to discuss the ways and means of achieving mortification until we recognize the *subject* of this duty. Here is a fundamental principle: Unless a man is a true believer—one who truly belongs to Christ—he can never mortify a single sin.

In Romans 8:13 Paul clearly implies this. "If ye [believers] through the Spirit do mortify the deeds of the body, ye shall live." Paul also says, "Mortify therefore your members which are upon the earth" (Col. 3:5). He is referring to those who are "risen with Christ" (3:1), to those who are "hid with Christ in God" (3:3). No unbeliever fits these descriptions.

You know the picture some of the Stoics and other philosophers, such as Seneca and Epictetus, drew about life. They discoursed about their contempt of the world and the self-life by their discipline and conquest of excessive emotions and passions. Yet their lives did not match their own maxims. Their self-sufficiency revealed their true nature. There is no death of sin without the death of Christ.

You also know the attempts some within the church have

made to discipline themselves by their vows, penances, and indulgences. Although they seek mortification, they never attain it. Why? "Because they seek it not by faith, but as it were by the works of the law" (Rom. 9:32). It is man's duty to mortify sin, but not in his own way.

The Spirit alone mortifies sin in believers. He has promised to do it, and all other means without Him are empty and vain. "If any man have not the Spirit of Christ, he is none of his" (Rom. 8:9). "So then they that are in the flesh cannot please God" (8:8). But those who have the Spirit of Christ are not in the flesh (see 8:9). By our union with Christ, mortification is accomplished (see 8:11). Let us reflect on several conclusions from these Scriptures.

1. Mortification is not possible for unregenerate man.

He needs to be converted. You would laugh at a builder who put up a structure without laying the foundation first. In Acts 2 the Jews, convicted of their sins, asked, "What shall we do?" (2:37). What did Peter tell them? Did he tell them to mortify pride, anger, malice, cruelty, and the like? No, he knew their existing condition and called them to conversion and faith in Christ (see 2:38). Humiliation under the cross comes first; then mortification follows. Unless a man is regenerate, all attempts he makes toward mortification fail.

Without regeneration, a man focuses his concern on those things that are not essential for him. He must first be brought home to God and then awakened to his whole condition, not just distracted to think of some discipline or some evident need in his own life. God speaks of Ephraim who returned "but not to the Most High" (Hos. 7:16). The people set themselves to relinquish sin, but not by the conversion they needed first. People became distracted from coming to God by their own self-imposed spiritual disciplines.

Moreover, if people have achieved peace of conscience or some other result from their disciplinary efforts, they tend to think the whole matter has been dealt with and solved. By such means, people satisfy themselves about their state and condition and become hardened by their self-righteousness. Later they discover they have not mortified sin, and then they despair that they can ever change. They find it even becomes easier to yield themselves up to the power and reality of sin in their lives.

This is the usual consequence for persons who attempt mortification of sin without first receiving Christ. First, sin deludes them, then hardens them, and then ultimately destroys them.

To kill sin is the work of living men. When men are dead (as all unbelievers, even the best of them, are dead), then sin is alive and will continue to flourish.

2. Mortification is the work of faith.

Mortification is the distinctive work of faith. It is faith that purifies the heart (see Acts 15:9). Peter says, we "purify our souls in obeying the truth through the Spirit" (1 Peter 1:22). Be sure to trust and depend upon Christ if you intend to mortify any sin. Without this, mortification will never take place.

You may object and say, "Well then, would you encourage unregenerate people to be convinced of the evil of sin? Is it not better to leave them alone? Is there any point in dissuading them from their dissolute lives and letting their lusts have full swing?" God forbid! Because of God's wisdom, goodness, and love, He chooses in many different ways to restrain men from more vileness and depravity than they already have. It is the goodness of God that the earth is not more of a hell of sin and confusion than it is already.

God's Word is still effective in the lives of people to challenge and humble them, even though they remain unconverted. Continue to preach the Word for the restraint of evil. Nevertheless, to those who do not receive it, the gall of bitterness remains. They still live in darkness. Moreover, let people know it is their duty to discipline their lives. Plead with them to realize their condition and show them what they need. But it is impossible to break off their particular sins without also breaking their hearts. It is grievous to see spiritual leaders lay heavy burdens of discipline upon poor souls who have a zeal for God and desire to possess eternal welfare. These burdens are misguided endeavors of mortification if they are performed in utter ignorance of the righteousness of Christ.

MORTFICATION REQUIRES OBEDIENCE

Mortification, then, is only for true believers. But not all believers can experience it in their present state. Without obedience to God, no believer can mortify sin. We cannot focus on a besetting sin, to destroy it, if we disobey God's commandments to us. This is a second general principle of mortification.

Suppose someone earnestly desires to mortify sin. He prays, sighs, groans, and longs for deliverance. Meanwhile, he neglects his devotional reading, his prayer life, his meditations with God. Then he wonders why sin retains its power in his life. This is a common condition among men.

The Israelites, under a sense of sin, drew near to God with much diligence and earnestness in prayer and fasting. "They seek me daily, and delight to know my ways ... they ask of me the ordinances of justice; they take delight in approaching to God" (Isa. 58:2). Yet God rejected it all. Their fastings could not heal them because, while they were particular in that duty, they were careless about others. The Israelites had an ulcerous wound they could never heal themselves, for they never hated sin as sin. Their blindness proceeded from self-love.

Without obedience to all of God's Word and all of God's provisions for salvation, isolated acts of mortification avail little. Universal obedience is essential. The apostle urges us, "Cleanse yourselves from all pollution of the flesh and spirit, perfecting holiness in the fear of God" (2 Cor. 7:1). Hating one particular sin or weakness is not enough; we must have a general disposition of life before God. The outbreak of one particular sin may only be symptomatic of a general condition of sickness, for sin lies at the root of our being. Thus God allows one sin to perplex us and gain strength over us in order to chasten us and allow us to see lukewarmness before the Lord.

Indeed, the rage and dominance of a particular lust or sin in us commonly results from a careless, negligent course of life. Lust lies in the heart of every one of us. While we keep diligent watch, it does not dominate over us. But when we let down our guard, it takes over.

God sometimes chastens us to keep us from greater sin. Thus the messenger of Satan buffeted Paul after he descended from his experience of the third heaven, "lest [he] should be exalted above measure through the abundance of the revelations" (2 Cor. 12:7). In mercy God corrected Paul of his vain confidence lest he fall into worse sin. We cannot resist God's chastening if we desire to mortify sin. We only obtain mortification of sin in one area of life as we remain open to the need of mortification in every area.

CHAPTER 15

THE PREPARATION FOR MORTIFICATION

We have considered two general rules of mortification so far. First, mortification comprises only the work of God in believers. Second, mortification implies obedience without reservation. Let us now consider several practical directions needed to mortify a particular sin that affects us.

1. Consider whether the sin exhibits particularly dangerous symptoms.

If a sin is especially deadly, you will need extraordinary remedies to deal with it. An ordinary course of mortification will never do. "What," you ask, "are these dangerous symptoms?" We can name some of them.

First, look for a sense of inevitability about the sin. If this lust has long lain in the heart, corrupting it, and its power and prevalence have been allowed to develop without strong efforts to deal with it, then such a soul sickness becomes serious. Perhaps it has been permitted through worldliness, ambition, or even studies, to dominate over other duties for a long time—especially over communion with God. Perhaps a filthy imagination has been indulged in for a long time. David confessed, "My wounds stink and are corrupt because of my foolishness" (Ps. 38:5). When a sin has lain for a long time in corrupting lust, it festers the soul and brings it to a very sorry state.

In such a condition, ordinary humiliation and a sense of shame will not be enough. It has crept its way into the mind and conscience far too deeply to be easily eradicated. It may be that the soul has tried both mercies and afflictions to remove it, but it persists like an old wound. This is a dangerous condition indeed.

Second, scrutinize the special pleas you make to excuse and tolerate a sin within you. We tend to overlook a dominant sin and to see what good traits we have in compensation. It is indeed good for us to seek communion with God and to call God to mind in our experiences. David says, "I commune with mine own heart" about God's dealings (Ps. 77:6). This is a discipline Paul urges us to practice (see 2 Cor. 13:5). But it can also be a terrible delusion when we overlook the need of repentance and of mortification against sin and instead cover it all up with a false pietism. The Jews called themselves "Abraham's children" and assumed God accepted their practices, in spite of Christ's preaching against them.

To apply grace and mercy to an unmortified sin, or not to deal sincerely with it, is fraudulent indeed. It is like the argument of Naaman: "In all other things I will walk with God, but in this one thing God be merciful to me" (2 Kings 5:18). To indulge in sin in the hope of mercy is inconsistent with Christian sincerity; it is the badge of hypocrisy. It is "turning the grace of our God into wantonness" (Jude 4). We must beware of tolerating these forms of deceit within us.

Third, note the frequency with which sin eludes mortification. This occurs when the will enjoys the sin and goes along with it secretly, even if it does nothing outwardly wrong. It also occurs when we are not vigilant and watchful or when we continue to show negligence about sin when it surprises us.

Fourth, determine if you argue against sin only because you

fear punishment. If you do, it is evident that you have already succumbed to it. The fear of shame before men or of punishment from God indicates no real concern to deal directly with the sin or lust. Those who are Christ's, and who act in obedience upon gospel principles, behave very differently. They have the reality of the death of Christ, the love of Christ, the detestation of sin, and communion with God to reinforce them in their abhorrence of sin as sin. If "the love of Christ constrains us" (2 Cor. 5:14), then we will oppose any seduction of sin.

Restraining grace may keep us from ruin, but it is renewing grace that we need to give us a new spirit to deal with sin and to mortify it. Paul argues that sin will not have dominion over believers when they realize they are "not under the law, but under grace" (Rom. 6:14). Legal fears and motives are not enough to keep the defenses of the soul.

Fifth, watch lest God's chastening punishment hardens your heart. The Jews asked, "Why have you hardened us from the fear of your name?" (Isa. 63:17). This is sometimes God's way of dealing with unregenerate men. At times God also allows a new sin to introduce new afflictions of soul in order to bring an old sin to remembrance again. Is it possible that you have received special mercy, or protection, or deliverance from God, yet have failed to hearken and reform? If so, awake and realize your need.

Sixth, take heed lest sin turns your heart from God. It is a condition described by Isaiah: "For the iniquity of his covetousness was I angry, and smote him: I hid myself, and was wroth, and he went on stubbornly in the way of his heart" (Isa. 57:17). This is a tragic situation. If a man reads the Word of God or hears it preached, he may repent. But if his sins have such a hold upon him that, instead of relinquishing the evil in his heart, he turns against God, then his soul is in a sad condition indeed.

Consider whether the sin or lust with which you are contending has any of these dangerous symptoms associated with it. If so, our Savior's words are appropriate: "This kind goeth not out but by prayer and fasting" (Matt. 17:21). Remember as well that while these symptoms may occur in true believers, they are not characteristic of the true Christian. A man is not a believer because, like David, he is an adulterer. A wise man wounded by sin may do foolish things. He may confess, "If I am a believer, I am a most miserable one." But a true believer does not rely on how sinful he may act, but on the gospel principles of grace for his salvation.

2. Maintain a clear and abiding sense of guilt, danger, and evil of sin.

First, consider the *guilt* of sin. Do not be like Naaman, who tried to extenuate his guilt of compromising worship in the house of Rimmon (see 2 Kings 5:18). To argue that a sin is bad, but not as bad as it might be, is a poor spirit. All the tumult, perplexities, treacheries, and false hopes of sin lead to confusion of understanding. But do not make this an excuse for sin.

The foolish in the book of Proverbs are those who, like the young man enticed by the harlot, are "void of understanding" (Prov. 7:7). In his folly, he did not know that it would cost him his life (see 7:23). He did not realize the seriousness of his sin. In Hosea, the Lord describes Ephraim as "a silly dove without heart" (7:11). Ephraim did not understand his miserable condition.

Make a right judgment about the guilt of sin. To "continue in sin," argues the apostle, is not "that grace may abound" (Rom. 6:1–2). On the contrary, grace is given that sin will not abound any longer. Moreover, God, who sees the hearts of men, knows that hidden sin in the heart may be worse than open sins. So be alert to the seriousness of sin, for even when it is not overt and visible, it is quietly excusing itself while gathering strength in our lives.

Second, consider the *danger* of sin. One such danger is the hardening of the soul by the deceitfulness of sin (see Heb. 3:12–13). The hardening meant here by the apostle is obduracy. Once tenderhearted, some become rock hard—"sermon-proof and sickness-proof." Once they trembled before God's Word and presence, before thoughts of death, and before other realities. Now their heart is unaffected, with no thoughts of God's grace, mercy, or love. Their heart is hardened, their conscience seared, their mind blinded, their affections stupefied, and their whole soul deceived.

A further danger is the great correction of God that the Scripture calls His "vengeance," "judgment," or "punishment." We may shrink from the thought that He should do it, but there are times when He does. Beware and fear above all the hardness of your heart.

Loss of peace and strength is another threat to the soul. To have peace with God and to have strength to walk before Him—these are the great promises of the covenant of grace. In these we find life for our soul. Without them in some comfortable measure, our life is reduced to death. This is clearly the case with David. How often he complains of his disquieted soul, his grievous wounds, on this account. God says to His people, "I will leave them, hide my face, and what will become of their peace and strength?" (see Lam. 3:1, 18).

The final threat is, of course, eternal destruction. The Scriptures clearly indicate continuance in sin leads to eternal destruction. To persist under the power of sin is to incur destruction and everlasting separation from God (see Heb. 3:12; 10:38). It is the rule of God's proceedings with man. If a man departs from God and draws back through unbelief,

God's soul has no pleasure in him; destruction is the end result (see Gal. 6:8).

But some will say, "What of the assurance that 'there is now no condemnation to them that are in Christ Jesus'?" (Rom. 8:1). This is the assurance of those who "walk after the Spirit, and not after the flesh" (Rom. 8:1). "True," you argue, "but who is to know the comfort of this assertion? Who may assume it for himself?" God's judgment is twofold: of a man's person and of a man's ways. It is the judgment of a man's ways that we have been speaking about, not of his person. We have to mark our ways to avoid this judgment. If someone thinks that he will be damned, this conclusion should arouse him to mend his ways before God. This is not a judgment, however, that any man can make about another, other than as a warning to avoid the danger of its possibility.

Third, consider the *evil* of sin. While danger concerns what is future, evil concerns what exists in the present. Presently, sin grieves the Holy Spirit. And we are exhorted to "grieve not the holy Spirit of God, whereby ye are sealed unto the day of redemption" (Eph. 4:30). If by our ingratitude, we grieve a tender and loving friend, what more is it to grieve the tender, loving Spirit of God who has chosen our hearts as His dwelling place? "He does not afflict willingly nor grieve us" (Lam. 3:33). Will we daily grieve Him?

Moreover, the Lord Jesus Christ is wounded afresh by the evil of sin. His love is foiled. His enemy is gratified. To harbor sin is to "crucify the Son of God afresh, and put Him to an open shame" (Heb. 6:6).

The evil of sin also takes away a man's usefulness in his generation. His works, his endeavors, his labors seldom receive blessing from God. If he is a preacher, God will commonly blow upon his ministry and make it unprofitable. The world is full today of poor, withering professors of the faith. How few walk in the beauty and glory of the Lord! How barren and useless is so much public ministry! Among the many reasons for this, clearly one is the secret harboring of sin.

Sin saps a person's obedience to God like a worm at the roots of a plant. Sin deters all the graces of God. How vital it is for us to keep alive the considerations of the guilt, the danger, and the evil of sin. Dwell on their seriousness. Make them a powerful reality in your soul.

3. Let the guilty weight of sin burden your conscience.

Begin by bringing into your conscience the awareness of the rectitude and holiness of the law. Ponder on the law's holiness, spirituality, burning severity, inwardness, and absolute character. See, then, how you stand before it. Reflect on the terror of the Lord and how He will righteously judge each of your sins. Probably your conscience will seek to avoid its severe challenge, saying you are free from its condemnation. While you admit you do not measure up to it as you should, yet you do not feel troubled about it.

However, remind your conscience that as long as you have unmortified sin lurking in your heart, you are not free from the law's condemnation. If the law claims its full rule over you, you are condemned. Clearly, anyone who is evasive about this in his inner being, in order to indulge in secret sin, has no security on the basis of the gospel. He is not as free as he pretends. Whatever the issue, the law has the authority of God to seize such transgressions and bring them before His throne. Either you plead for pardon, or else you face judgment.

The proper work of the law is to reveal sin as utterly sinful in order to arouse and humble the soul. If you deny it, then you only show the hardness of your heart and the deceitfulness of sin. This is how professors of faith become apostate. They profess to be delivered from the law. Little by little this begins to influence them in practical ways and to possess them to such an extent that their will and affections turn to all manner of evil things.

Persuade your conscience to listen diligently to all that the law says about your lust and corruption. If you will ever mortify your sins, it must be as your conscience arms itself with a clear and thorough apprehension of the law. Like David, let your iniquity be ever before you (Ps. 51:3).

Force your lust to face the gospel, not for relief but for further conviction of its guilt. Look to Him whom you have pierced, and be in bitterness. Say to your soul, "What have I done? What love, what blood, what grace have I despised and trampled on? Is this the return I make to the Father for His love, to the Son for His shed blood, to the Holy Spirit for His grace? Is this how I requite the Lord? Have I defiled the heart that Christ died to wash, that the blessed Spirit has chosen to dwell in? What, then, can I say to my dear Lord Jesus? Do I account communion with Him of so little value? How shall I escape if I neglect such a great salvation? I have despised love, mercy, grace, goodness, peace, joy, consolation. I have despised them all as a thing of naught that I might persist in sin. Shall I daily grieve the Spirit whereby I am sealed to the day of redemption?"

From these general considerations, proceed to examine particular cases of your guilt before God. First, consider the infinite patience and forbearance of God toward you. Consider how He could have exposed and shamed you for all the ways you have dealt treacherously with Him, flattering Him with your lips but breaking your promises and commitments. Yet He has spared you time after time. Will you still persist in sinning against Him? Will you weary Him and make Him serve your corruptions? Have you not considered that it is utterly impossible He should tolerate your ways any longer? Is it not possible that all His patience with you is exhausted? Yet in spite of your deserved judgment, He has returned your evil with His love.

Second, reflect how often your heart has been on the brink of being hardened by the deceitfulness of sin, and yet by the infinitely rich grace of God you have been restored to communion with Him once more. Think of how your spiritual life has so often declined, so that your delight in spiritual disciplines, your obedience to His Word, and your prayer and meditation have slackened. At the same time, your inclinations to careless walk have increased, and you have been indulgent in keeping the kind of company God abhors. Will you venture yet nearer to the brink of such hardness of heart?

Third, reflect also on all the providential ways God has dealt with you in deliverances, in afflictions, in mercies, and in blessings. Load your conscience with these and repent before God. For unless the conscience is unable to alleviate its guilt of sin, the soul will never seriously attempt mortification.

4. Seek with a constant longing to be delivered from the power of sin.

Do not allow your heart to be content with the status quo for one moment. In the natural and material realm, longing desires are useless unless they are reinforced by a diligent exercise to fulfill them. But with spiritual things it is otherwise. Longing, breathing, and panting after deliverance is a grace in itself, having a mighty power to conform the soul to the likeness of the thing longed after. The apostle, describing the repentance and godly sorrow of the Corinthians, speaks of this as "vehement desire" (2 Cor. 7:11). In the context of speaking about indwelling sin in

Romans 7, he breaks out in longing desire to be rid of it. Unless we long for deliverance, we will never have it.

This longing will make us watchful for any opportunity to gain the advantage over the enemy and ready for every assistance to destroy it. Strong desires for deliverance give life to "praying without ceasing"—a command enjoined upon us in all conditions, and none more important than this (1 Thess. 5:17). These desires will have done their work when the soul once again seeks after God. Remember the example of David. Set your heart with this frame of desire, with sighs and crying.

5. Consider if the evil perplexing you is rooted in your nature and nurtured and exaggerated by your temperament.

A proneness to a particular sin may lie in one's natural character and disposition. This argument is not in the least an excuse to extenuate the guilt of your sin. Some people will, with open profanity, cheerfully blame the most serious crimes to their natural instinct and tendencies of character. I suppose that others may do so more secretly.

But we have to remember it was from the fall of man, from the original deprivation of our nature, that sin entered our lives. It is only the shape and nourishment of our sins that our natural dispositions reflect. David reckons he is "shapen in iniquity" and "conceived in sin" (Ps. 51:5). Thus his falling into sin only exaggerates the original condition of his life. That you are peculiarly inclined toward a certain sin is cause for personal humility.

In walking with God, you have to fix attention clearly on this prevailing tendency. Otherwise, it will always be a weakness that Satan can exploit to full advantage. Many find themselves rushed and swept along the path to hell because of this weakness, when otherwise they would go at a gentler pace.

There is only one solution to this problem. Paul says, "I keep under my body, and bring it into subjection" (1 Cor. 9:27). This is an ordinance for the mortification of sin. This gives a check to the natural disposition to sin. The Roman Catholic tradition has overexaggerated this in their ignorance of the righteousness of Christ and the work of His Holy Spirit, stressing mortification in voluntary acts and penances. But perhaps Protestants have ventured too far the other way and neglected this means of mortification that God has ordained that we should use. Bringing the body into subjection by such means as watching our diet, fasting, and the like, is acceptable to God. But remember they have two limitations.

First, do not think the outward weakening and curbing of bodily appetites is a good in itself. Nor think mortification consists of such acts. A man can be lean in both body and soul!

Second, guard against the idea that the method of dieting or fasting has power in itself to give virtue. It cannot give true mortification of sin. If it could, then any unregenerate person in the world could mortify sin without the help of the Holy Spirit. We must consider methods only as ways and means the Holy Spirit uses to accomplish His work in us, when sin is rooted in our natural disposition and temperament.

6. Watch out for the occasions when your evil sickness tends to occur.

This is one aspect of the duty that our Savior commends to His disciples: "I say unto you, Watch" (Mark 13:37). Take heed, or your hearts will be weighed down (Luke 21:34). Look out for any eruptions of your corruptions. This is what David recognized when he said, "I have kept myself from mine iniquity" (Ps. 18:23). He watched for all ways and means by which his iniquity was likely to rise up against him. In this way he could prevent it.

This is what the Lord calls us to do when He says, "Consider your ways" (Hag. 1:5, 7). Consider what company, what opportunities, what businesses, and what situations most likely will bring about this sickness of evil within us. We do this with regard to our own bodily sicknesses. We watch out for the seasons, or the conditions, or the diet that we should avoid. Are the things of the soul of less importance? Why do we neglect these spiritual realities?

Hazael did not think he could possibly act as wickedly as the prophet told him he would act. To convince him, the prophet simply said, "You shall be the king of Syria" (2 Kings 8:13). In other words, Hazael would act cruelly if he ventured into areas where he would be tempted to act cruelly. Likewise, if we tell someone that he might commit such and such sin, he would be shocked and reject such an accusation. But if you go on to show him the situations and occasions for these temptations, he will have little grounds for confidence in rejecting these suggestions.

7. React strongly against the first stirrings of your evil disposition.

Do not allow it to get the least start in your life. Do not say, "I will let it go so far, but no further." If you allow it to have one step, it will take another, for it is impossible to fix limits on sin. It is like water in a channel; if it breaks out, it will follow its own course. This is how James describes the process of lust by stages in James 1:14–15.

Rise up with all your strength against the first suggestion of sin, and be no less indignant about it than if it had already accomplished its aims. Consider what an evil thought it is that involved you in filth and foolishness. Ask envy what it would have; murder and destruction are its aims. Set yourself against it with no less vigor than if it had already involved you in its final desires. Without this course, you will never prevail, for if sin gets grounded within the affections, it becomes much more difficult for the understanding to cope with it.

8. Use meditation as a means of self-abasement by contemplating God's perfection and your sinfulness.

Meditate on the excellence of God's majesty and your own infinite, inconceivable distance from Him. This will prompt you to recognize your evil heart, a recognition that strikes at the root of any indwelling sin within you.

Remember the experience of Job. When he clearly discerns the greatness and excellency of God, he is filled with self-abhorrence and forced down in humiliation (see Job 42:5–6). In what a similar condition is Habakkuk when he apprehends the majesty of God (see Hab. 3:16). Yes, says Job, "with God is terrible majesty" (Job 37:22). No wonder these witnesses of God thought they should die at the sight of Him. Scripture abounds with this perspective of men's puniness and vileness before the majesty of God. Men are "grasshoppers," "vanity," and "the small dust of the balance" in comparison to God (Isa. 40:12–28). Meditate much on this to abase the pride of your heart and to keep your soul humble within you.

Meditate much on your unacquaintedness with God. Little as you may know of Him, it is more than enough to keep you low and humbled. Even so, how little do you really know of God! Agur confesses, "Surely I am more brutish than any man, and have not the understanding of a man. I neither learned wisdom, nor have the knowledge of the holy. Who hath ascended up into heaven, or descended? Who hath gathered the wind in his fists? Who hath bound the waters in a garment? Who hath established all the ends of the earth? What is his name, and what is his son's name, if thou canst tell?" (Prov. 30:2–4).

Meditate deeply over this to take down the pride of your heart. What do you really know of God? How very small it is! Yet how immense He is! Can you look into the abyss of eternity without terror? No, you cannot bear the rays of His glorious reality.

I consider this kind of meditation of great value in our walk with God. But it must be consistently combined with a filial boldness, given us in Jesus Christ, to draw near to the throne of grace. Then it will make an abiding impression in our souls and give us a deep desire to walk humbly with God.

If we keep this attitude and meditation before us, we will see that the greatest saints—those nearest and most in communion with God—still have very little knowledge of God and His glory in this life. God revealed His name to Moses proclaiming His most glorious attributes (see Exod. 34:5–7). Yet these were still but "the back parts" of God (33:23). Moses knew very little compared with the perfection of God's glory. Hence it is with specific reference to Moses that it is said, "No man hath seen God at any time" (John 1:18). This also applies to the incarnation of Christ, whom men could see—but only in part.

We speak of God, His ways, His works, His counsels all day long. But the truth is we know very little of God. Our thoughts, our meditations, our expressions of Him are low; many are quite unworthy of His glory, and none reach to His perfections.

You may argue, "Since Moses was under the law, wrapped in darkness and clouded with types and institutions, he could not see God. But under the glorious light of the gospel of Christ, who 'hath brought life and immortality to light,' God has now revealed Himself more fully see (2 Tim. 1:10). We see Him much more clearly. Now we can see His face, whereas Moses could only see His back."

Of course, I acknowledge the vast and inconceivable difference between the acquaintance we have with God now that He has spoken to us by His own Son (see Heb. 1:2) and that which the saints had under the law. Yet even that vision of God that Moses had was a gospel vision, for he saw God as gracious and merciful (see Exod. 34:6–7). True, we now see "with open face, beholding as in a glass the glory of the Lord" (2 Cor. 3:18). Yet it is "through a glass, darkly" (1 Cor. 13:12); it is seeing "the back parts of God" (Exod. 33:23).

We know how weak, feeble, and uncertain children comprehend truth. Yet we are but children still in our comprehension of God. In spite of all our pretensions, we only babble and lisp when we speak of Him. Like the queen of Sheba, we think we know a great deal. Yet seeing Solomon, she had to admit, "Behold, the one half of the greatness of thy wisdom was not told me: for thou exceedest the fame that I heard" (2 Chron. 9:6; 1 Kings 10:7). Indeed, the apostle says we do not even know "what we shall be" (1 John 3:2). How then can we fully know the eternal God?

Meditate on the reality that if God is only to be known as God, the attributes we ascribe to Him are fully inadequate. We describe Him as immortal and infinite, perhaps because we know man is mortal and finite. Paul says, "Christ only hath immortality, dwelling in the light which no man can approach unto; whom no man hath seen, nor can see" (1 Tim. 6:16). As we cannot look into the sun with the naked eye, no more can we look upon the Creator of the sun. We lose all sense of understanding in the presence of God.

Meditate, nevertheless, on the being of God. We are so removed from a knowledge of God that we readily make idols of the mind out of the very words we use to talk about God. Just as men readily cut down a tree trunk and fashion an idol out of it, so we can make an idol of the mind out of our theological speculations. It is a god of our own making, not the God who made us. Our utmost thoughts about God only acknowledge that we can have no satisfactory thoughts about Him.

Still, there are some things God has taught us about Himself. But we do not know them directly. All we can do is believe and admire them. We believe God is everywhere, infinite, and all-powerful, and we debate about what such ideas mean. Yet the very notions are beyond our comprehension, let alone the God whom we so describe. Is then our knowledge not brutish in comparison to God? Thank God, we know Him much more by what He does than by who He is. Job knew God better by what He did for him in His goodness than by His essential goodness. We only see a little portion of His ways, but we can realize them in our experience.

It follows that if God is known by what He does, then it is by faith alone that we know God. "He that cometh to God must believe that he is, and that he is a rewarder of them that diligently seek him" (Heb. 11:6). We know God by believing. "We walk by faith, not by sight" (2 Cor. 5:7). Faith is the certainty of "things not seen" (Heb. 11:1).

Some may argue, "All this is true, but has Christ not made a difference? 'No man hath seen God at any time; the only begotten Son which is in the bosom of the Father, he hath declared him' (John 1:18). We now have 'the glorious gospel of Christ, who is the image of God' shining in our hearts (2 Cor. 4:4, 6). 'We all, with open face behold ... the glory of the Lord' (2 Cor. 3:18). Once in darkness, we now live in light (Eph. 5:8)."

Yes, indeed, the knowledge we have of God by the revelation of Jesus Christ is exceedingly glorious. But the truth is we all know enough of God to love Him, to delight in Him, to serve Him, to believe Him, to obey Him, and to put our trust in Him more than we actually do. Likewise, the difference between believers and unbelievers is not so much in the *matter* of their knowledge of God as in the *manner* of their knowledge. The excellency of a believer does not consist in how much he knows, but in what he assimilates and what becomes transformed within his soul.

To meditate upon God in the gospel is not to unveil His essential glory, that we should see Him as He is. Rather, it is to declare as much of God as He knows is sufficient to form the foundation for our faith, love, obedience, and coming to Him. That is the faith He expects of us here in the world. But when He calls us to eternal admiration and contemplation, He will give us a new discovery of Himself. Then this whole semblance of things, as it now appears, will depart as a shadow before the light of His eternal presence.

Yes, we are dull and slow of heart to receive the things God's Word reveals even though they are so clear and evident. God, by our infirmity and weakness, keeps us in continual dependence upon Him for teachings and revelation of Himself from His Word. Never in this world does He bring any soul to the utmost of what is discoverable and recognizable from the Word. Let us, then, discerning once more the awful distance between the inconceivably great God and our own smallness, fill our soul with a holy and awesome fear of Him.

9. Take care that you do not speak peace to yourself before God speaks it.

Hearken to what God says to your soul. This is a matter of vital importance in light of all the warnings God gives to us of self-deception, of the deceitfulness of sin, and of carelessness. Let us note two basic principles.

First, it is the prerogative and the sovereignty of God to give grace to whom He pleases. "He has mercy on whom He will have mercy" (Rom. 9:18). Among all the sons of men, He calls whom He wills and sanctifies when He wills. It is a privilege He reserves for Himself.

Second, it is the sovereign grace of God to speak peace to the conscience. Just as God creates and chooses, so He also "comforts" (Isa. 57:18). God alone declares real peace to the soul. It is His prerogative to do so. Christ says, "I am the Amen, the faithful witness," in contrast to the Laodicean church, who sought to heal her wounds falsely and speak peace to herself (see Rev. 3:14).

Let us then establish some rules by which men may authentically speak peace. The first is this: *Men cannot speak peace to themselves who have not also detested their own sins*. Men wounded by sin must realize healing only comes in the redemptive work of Christ. This produces contrition and repentance; they can calm their souls in Christ. When men "look upon [Him] whom they have pierced" and mourn, then they will detest the sins that so pierced Him (Zech. 12:10). When we see that "the chastisement of our peace was upon him; and with his stripes we are healed" (Isa. 53:5), then we find healing and peace in Him and Him alone.

God in His new covenant of grace says, "I will establish unto thee an everlasting covenant" (Ezek. 16:60). What then? "Then thou shalt remember thy ways, and be ashamed" (16:61). The shame that our sins have alienated us from God is a godly sorrow that leads us to repentance and salvation. Like Job, we can have no abiding peace until we abhor ourselves (see Job 42:6).

The psalmist describes the lack of peace of those whose "heart was not right with him, neither were they stedfast" (Ps. 78:37). It is impossible to have true peace of conscience and a right relationship with God without dealing with the realities of indwelling sin and recognizing the seriousness of such sin in our lives. Without mortification, you will have little peace in this life, and instead remain sick and fainting all your days.

The second rule is this: *When men are at peace with themselves on the basis of their own convictions and rational principles, their peace is false and will not abide.*

Someone realizes all is not well with his relationship to God. He knows what to do to put it right. He seeks the promises of God to heal his soul and calm his heart, and he applies each like a bandage to a wound. But he does so merely in an intellectual, rational manner. This is the natural man at work ... the enlightened natural man. But it is not the work of the Spirit, who alone convinces us "of sin, and of righteousness, and of judgment" (John 16:8). True spiritual life is not then the principle of this man's actions. He does not act in the strength of the Holy Spirit, neither are his fruits from that root.

It is like someone in distress who finds the promise, "The Lord will have mercy, and our God will abundantly pardon" (Isa. 55:7). Or he reads, "I will heal their backsliding, I will love them freely" (Hos. 14:4). But he does not allow the Spirit of God to apply this to his own state. He does not wait upon God. He does not listen to God speaking to Him. He merely rationalizes from the Scriptures what he wants to apply naturally.

"How then," you may ask, "can we really know that we are not doing the same thing?" The promise is given, "The meek will he guide in judgment: and the meek will he teach his way" (Ps. 25:9). So wait upon the Lord. This means that we apply only the grace and that distinct act of faith that God calls for in our situation. The prophet says, "I will wait upon the LORD, who hideth his face from the house of Jacob" (Isa. 8:17). He waits patiently on the Lord.

What do the self-healers do instead? First, they do not wait for God to assure their hearts with His peace. They dictate their own peace. Momentarily, the false peacemakers may have rest of conscience, but it does not last. It does not sweeten their hearts.

Second, what is worse, this false peace does not assure the life and heal the evil. When God speaks peace, the soul "turns not again to folly" (Ps. 85:8). It does not cover the wound with a bandage; it completely heals. It gives such sweetness and such a discovery of God's love, that the soul is strongly obligated never to deal crookedly and perversely again.

Third, to speak peace to ourselves is to do so superficially. "They have healed also the hurt of the daughter of my people slightly," complains the prophet (Jer. 6:14). The apostle speaks of those who heard the message without profit, because they did not combine it with faith (see Heb. 4:2). We cannot merely look or glance at the Word; we must receive it in faith. Without this, our wounds heal superficially only to break out again.

Fourth, when man speaks peace to himself when he has none, he has not really settled accounts with God. God is "of purer eyes than to behold iniquity" (Hab. 1:13). When a man does not repent or deal with his sin, he cannot experience real peace in his soul. He probably has other sins he has not faced, such as worldliness, pride, or some other concealed folly.

Finally, when men speak peace to their consciences, it is seldom that God speaks humility to their souls. God's peace is a humbling peace, as it was in the case of David (see Ps. 51:1). Now God may speak peace to our hearts immediately after we have sinned and repented, or He may wait and speak later.

How shall we know when God really does speak peace to our hearts? Faith knows His voice. "The sheep follow him: for they know his voice" (John 10:4). If you keep close to God in acquaintance and communion with Him, you will always know the voice of God and distinguish it from that of a stranger. When He speaks, it makes your "heart burn within you" (Luke 24:32). He does so by "putting in his hand by the hole of the door" (Song 5:4). In other words, the Spirit grips your heart.

We also recognize God's Word by the way it humbles, cleanses, and performs what it promises. Its promise is to endear, to melt, and to bind us in obedience as we wait upon God and empty ourselves before Him.

CHAPTER 16

THE PRACTICE OF MORTIFICATION

The considerations that I have insisted upon are only preparatory for the work of mortification. It is the heart's preparation for the work that I have aimed to present to you. The directions for the actual work of mortification are very few. Indeed, there are only two. The first is to live wholly and solely in your trust of Christ. The second is to seek the Holy Spirit, who alone mortifies sin.

TRUST IN THE SUFICIENCY OF CHRIST

Avoid the entanglements of lust by filling your soul with the realization of all the provisions available in Christ Jesus. Moreover, ponder that you are in no way able, in and by yourself, to contend against your sinful condition. When you are weary of the struggle and ready to give up, there is always enough in Jesus Christ to give you relief (see Phil. 4:13). It sustained the prodigal—when he was ready to faint and yet a great way off—to know that there was "bread enough and to spare" in his father's house (Luke 15:17). Likewise, consider the treasure of strength, might, and help at our disposal (see Isa. 40:28–31) and for our support in Christ (see John 1:16; Col. 1:19).

To act in faith on the fullness that is in Christ to supply all our needs is a wonderful way of abiding in Christ. Let your soul declare: "I am a poor weak thing; unstable as water, I cannot excel spiritually. The corruption of the flesh is too hard for me to cope with by myself. I have been deceived too many times to believe that I have finally obtained victory over sin. I am tempted to say, 'My way is hid from the LORD, and my judgment is passed over from my God.' Yet I know that 'the everlasting God, the LORD, the Creator of the ends of the earth, fainteth not, neither is weary ... there is no searching of his understanding. He giveth power to the faint, and to them that have no might he increaseth strength'" (Isa. 40:27–29). He assures us that His grace is sufficient (see 2 Cor. 12:9).

Raise your expectations of what Christ can do for you. "As the eyes of servants look unto the hand of their masters" (Ps. 123:2), so we can expect Christ's help. The disciples asked, "To whom can we go?" (John 6:68). Christ says, "Without me ye can do nothing" (John 15:5). When we are strengthened with power in our inner being, it is so that Christ may dwell in our hearts by faith (Eph. 3:16–17). In Him alone "all fulness dwells" (Col. 1:19). It is "of his fulness that we receive grace for grace" (John 1:16). All other ways and resources to which we may direct our expectations are futile and invalid.

As we direct our expectations to Christ and to Him alone, we encounter His tenderness. He is our great High Priest at the right hand of God (see Heb. 4:14). "As one whom his mother comforts, so I will comfort you," says God (Isa. 66:13). He has the tenderness of a mother with a nursing child (see Ps. 131:2). "It behoved him in all things to be made like unto his brethren, that he might be a merciful and faithful high priest in all things pertaining to God, to make reconciliation for the sins of the people" (Heb. 2:17). How is Christ able to help us with such tenderness and understanding? Because in that "he himself hath suffered being tempted, he is able to succour them that are tempted" (2:18). He is moved to help us (see Heb. 4:15–16).

Consider also Christ's faithfulness. He has promised to help and to relieve our distresses. God compares His covenant with us to the ordinances of heaven—the laws that keep the sun, moon, and stars in their courses (see Jer. 31:35–36). David could anticipate God's faithfulness as one who watched for the morning (see Ps. 130:6); it was a daily, predictable event. Such is the relief that Christ promises, for He is faithful in what He has promised.

Expectant then of such help from Christ, the soul will ask Him for speedy and full assistance. Our Lord Jesus has raised our hearts in expectation of help by His kindness, care, and promises. Like the psalmist, we can declare, "Thou, LORD, hast not forsaken them that seek thee" (Ps. 9:10). Once the heart is at rest with Him, God will assuredly satisfy it. Christ will never fail us.

This encourages the heart to attend to all the ways and means whereby Christ communicates to the soul. Like a beggar, he must knock at the door for help. To receive Christ's help, we need to wait upon Him. It is the expectation in faith that sets the heart to work in the exercise of true prayer and meditation.

Focus your expectations of Christ upon the reality of His death and resurrection. Mortification is death; and Christ died for all. This is His purpose: "He gave himself for us, that he might redeem us from all iniquity, and purify unto himself a peculiar people, zealous of good works" (Titus 2:14). He gave Himself for the church "that he might sanctify and cleanse it ... that he might present it to himself a glorious church, not having spot, or wrinkle, or any such thing; but that it should be holy and without blemish" (Eph. 5:25–27). That is why our purging is related to His blood.

Act then in faith on the death of Christ, expecting its power in your life; conform to it in your spirit (see Phil. 3:10; Col. 3:3; 1 Peter 1:18–19).

SEEK THE HOLY SPIRIT FOR THE MORTFICATION OF SIN

The duty of mortification, as we have described it, is only accomplished through the Holy Spirit. He alone does the actual work.

First, the Holy Spirit clearly and fully convinces the heart of the evil and guilt that need to be mortified. Without His conviction, there would be no thorough work done. "He convinces of sin" (John 16:8). He alone can do this. If man's rational ability could do so, we might see more conviction of sin in the world. But this light is not powerful or reliable enough, as we have seen. Unless we are convinced of the unique power of the Holy Spirit, we shall go on living in futility about sin.

Second, the Holy Spirit alone reveals to us the fullness of Christ for our relief. It is this that will uphold the heart from false ways and from despondency.

Third, the Spirit alone establishes the heart in expectation of help from Christ. This is the great means of mortification, as we have discovered (see 2 Cor. 1:21).

Fourth, the Spirit alone brings the cross of Christ into our hearts with its sin-killing power. By the Spirit we are baptized into the death of Christ. By baptism we recognize the implantation of Christ's life in our souls, replacing our old, sinful self. The apostle writes, "Knowing this, that our old man is crucified with him, that the body of sin might be destroyed, that henceforth we should not serve sin" (Rom. 6:6).

Fifth, the Spirit is the author and finisher of our sanctification. He provides the resources and new influences of grace for holiness and sanctification. He does this when the contrary principle of the flesh is weakened (see Eph. 3:16–18).

Finally, in all the soul's relationships with God, we have the support of the Holy Spirit. Where else do we receive this power, life, and vigor of prayer? Where is our efficacy to prevail with God? Is it not from the Spirit? He is called "the Spirit of supplications," promised to those "who look on him whom they have pierced" (Zech. 12:10). It is the Spirit who "maketh intercession for us with groanings which cannot be uttered" (Rom. 8:26). The Spirit is the great go-between and the way for faith to prevail with God.

INDEX

SUBJECT INDEX

READERS' GUIDE

FOR PERSONAL REFLECTION OR GROUP DISCUSSION

READERS' GUIDE
INTRODUCTION

The Victor Classic series is committed to making accessible to today's readers the powerful Christian voices of past eras. And our hope is that as you read through this book, you will use the discussion points in the following pages to take you to an even deeper level of faith through personal challenge and application.

You can study these points on your own or in the context of a group study or course work for a class. Perhaps you will even invite a friend or a group of friends to work through the book with you. Our prayer is that you will let yourself be challenged to change the way you live based on the answers you discover to life's most pressing questions.

Introduction

1. In his introduction to John Owen's *Triumph Over Temptation*, J. I. Packer comments that "the living of the Christian life was his [Owen's] constant theme." Why does this theme appeal to you?

2. Owen viewed humankind as "created in God's image for rational action and equipped to that end with a trinity of faculties: understanding, will, and affection" (p. 23). How can believers reflect God's image by the way they process information? By the way they make decisions? By the way they handle their emotions?

Chapter One

1. This chapter insists the law of sin is in believers but is not a law to believers. What personal experiences confirm this contrasting truth in your life? How does this distinction help you empathize with fellow believers?

2. How does knowing that sin dwells deep in the human heart affect your concept of self-image? How does this knowledge affect your response to the popular belief that all human beings are essentially good? How does it deepen your appreciation of divine grace?

Chapter Two

1. John Owen portrays sin as constant enmity against God. What three biblical events most strikingly support this conclusion? What enmity against God do you see in contemporary world events?

2. What practical benefits in combating sin do you see in each of the following disciplines: respect for all of God's commandments, prayer, contrition, and spiritual worship?

3. God raises barriers to obstruct the path to sins. These are rational considerations and providential events (helpful circumstances). How does the fear of death, judgment, and hell obstruct the path to sins? What circumstances, negative or positive, might persuade a believer to turn away from sin?

Chapter Three

1. John Owen believed that "deceit is most often the origin of sinning." What deceptions lead to personal sins? Societal sins?

2. Read Philippians 4:8. Why is the personal application of this verse's instruction so important in the believer's battle with sin?

3. How does the deceitfulness of sin abuse the doctrine of grace? How would you respond to the suggestion that grace makes almost all behaviors okay?

4. What truths can you draw on to keep sin from deceiving you?

Chapter Four

1. According to John Owen, "sin always seeks to extenuate and lessen the seriousness of sin to the mind" (p. 100). What sins are sometimes excused by saying, "What's the harm?" or "What I do is nobody's business but mine" or "It's my body. I can do what I want with it"?

2. What positive actions can you take to refuse "the pleasures of sin"? How can you develop contempt for sin but a desire to please God?

Chapter Five

1. Our text contends that "moral actions are willed" (p. 105) and quotes an ancient sage's comment: "Every sin is so voluntary, that if it is not voluntary, it is not sin." Do you agree or disagree that all immorality occurs because the human will rejects God's will? For example, should we attribute homosexual behavior to a genetic cause or to a willful opposition to God's law? Defend your position.

2. In what ways do sinners try to alleviate their sense of guilt? What measures does God take to restrain sin?

Chapter Six

1. How do you explain the fact that occasionally a spiritual leader succumbs to scandalous behavior? What precautions can you take to safeguard your relationship with the Lord?

2. The media expose children early and often to immorality. Parents cannot insulate their children from every immoral image and word, but what actions can they take to counter such harmful exposure?

Chapter Seven

1. Every Christian admits that he or she should exercise prayerful vigilance. However, most Christians, like their unbelieving contemporaries, lead busy lives. What time-consuming interests compete for the attention you know you should devote to prayer? How will you adjust your schedule to allow for vigilant prayer?

2. The author acknowledges that God reveals Himself through trials. What recent trials has God used to reveal Himself to you? What did you learn about Him through those trials?

Chapter Eight

1. John Owen taught that facing temptation and being led into temptation are two distinct situations. How do you think these two situations differ? How is it possible to enter into temptation but not fall under temptation? (See page 144 for help.)

2. A warning is issued on page 146: "Be prepared for the time when temptation becomes strong." What measures can a believer take to heed this warning?

3. How did the forces of fear and allurement unite to destroy David's relationship with God? When sinful lusts lure us away from a close relationship with God, what fears tend to impede our willingness to forsake our sin?

Chapter Nine

1. John Owen argued strongly that no one lies beyond the power of temptation, and, therefore, no one should be confident that he or she will not fall to temptation. Although most Christians do not yield to temptations that cause public disgrace, we may fall victim to temptations that lead to personal, undisclosed sins. What personal, undisclosed sins do you believe most of us are prone to commit if we are not vigilant?

2. How might believers encourage one another to resist temptation? What steps should we take when a fellow believer "is caught in a sin" (Gal. 6:1)?

Chapter Ten

1. What temptations do you believe usually accompany fame and success? How might an admiring Christian public increase a famous person's risk of falling to temptation? How can we honor a successful Christian leader or author without unknowingly setting him or her up for a fall?

2. According to the author, "If we do not abide in prayer, we will abide in temptation" (p. 165). How can a twenty-first-century believer abide in prayer?

Chapter Eleven

1. This chapter insists believers face temptation in times of prosperity as well as at other times. What dangers might prosperity pose to Christians? What temptations might strike us in "lean" times?

2. We are advised on page 171 that "to avoid temptation," we each need to understand our natural temperament." Do you agree with this advice? Why or why not? What temptations might strike a self-confident person? A hard-driving person? An easygoing person? A highly emotional person? A soft-hearted person?

Chapter Twelve

1. "Patience must accompany the gospel" (p. 179). How does the "gospel," the Good News of Christ, inspire you to be patient in the midst of trials? When international tensions and strife escalate? When others misunderstand you or mistreat you?

2. No doubt, all Christians readily agree with the statement on page 186 that "God sees things differently from the world." By faith we perceive all of life through the lens of Scripture. How would you contrast the "faith perspective" with that of unbelievers with respect to each of the following: the meaning of life;

the value of possessions; the nature of sin; the attractiveness of Christ; security; and the future, including life after death?

Chapter Thirteen

1. How would you define "mortification" after reading John Owen's discussion of the mortification of sin? How do you distinguish between mortification of sin and the total elimination of sin?

2. Do you agree that John Owen viewed the believer's struggle with sin as a lifelong battle? If this struggle lasts a lifetime, how can a believer achieve daily victory over sin?

Chapter Fourteen

1. The second and third complete paragraphs on page 203 offer a strong condemnation of the person who merely professes faith but fails to mortify sin daily. Read these paragraphs again, and tell why you agree or disagree with John Owen's conclusions.

2. According to John Owen, the Holy Spirit mortifies sin, but we must cooperate with Him in this work (p. 204). How do you explain these distinct but interdependent roles?

3. How does divine chastening help us mortify sin? How can believers become more receptive to divine chastening?

Chapter Fifteen

1. Is it less than noble to oppose personal sin only because we fear its negative consequences? Explain. What do you see as noble reasons to oppose personal sins?

2. In general, do you think the Christian community is becoming tolerant of sin? Defend your answer. If you believe the Christian community is becoming more tolerant of sin, what needs to happen to reverse this tolerant attitude?

Chapter Sixteen

1. John Owen believed that mortification of sin occurs when believers "live wholly and solely" in their "trust of Christ" and "seek the Holy Spirit." How can believers in a high-tech, busy culture implement these two principles?

2. How does Christ's faithfulness encourage you to overcome sin and temptation?

3. After reading *Triumph Over Temptation*, what succinct advice might you give a new Christian who worries that he may not be able to lead a righteous life?

Additional copies of *Triumph Over Temptation*
and other Victor Classics titles
are available from your local Christian bookseller.

If you have enjoyed this book,
or if it has had an impact on your life,
we would like to hear from you.

Please contact us at:

Victor Books
Cook Communications Ministries, Dept. 201
4050 Lee Vance View
Colorado Springs, CO 80918

Or visit our Web site: www.cookministries.com

Victor®
The Bible Teacher's Teacher

Julian - Ankle
Jay Allen - Finger
Chris Fletcher - Finger
Amanda Smith - Dentist
Peter Connover - Shin

Shin

Jumpers knee?